CONNECTED
PARENT
EMPOWERED
CHILD

For Dawne

With all good
wishes on your path!

Warmly,

Teeya

A **CORE** SUCCESS™ GUIDE

CONNECTED PARENT EMPOWERED CHILD

Five Keys to Raising
Happy, Confident, Responsible Kids

LEEZA CARLONE STEINDORF

ILLUSTRE PRESS INTERNATIONAL

Library of Congress Control Number: 2015920229
Steindorf, Leeza Carlone
Connected Parent, Empowered Child: Five Keys to Raising Happy, Confident, Responsible Kids
ISBN 978-0-9969529-0-3 (softbound)
ISBN: 978-0-9969529-1-0 (e-book)

Published in the United States by
Illustre Press International
PO Box 219121
Portland, Oregon 97225

Books are available in quantity for promotional or premium use. For infor-mation on discounts and terms, write to: Director of Special Sales, Illustre Press International, PO Box 219121, Portland, Oregon 97225

Editing by Heidi Grauel and Judith Briles
Book Design by Jerry Dorris, AuthorSupport.com

*This work is dedicated to Dominik Tyler and Leah Lorén,
my master teachers and greatest blessings, and in memory of
Robert Carlone and Gloria Harmel, my honored way-showers.*

With gratefulness for the love that shines in, through and as us all.

Contents

Children do not magically learn morality, kindness and decency any more than they learn math, English or science. They mature into decent and responsible people by emulating adults who are examples and models for them, especially courageous parents with principles and values who stand up for what they believe.

Raising Your Child to be a Mensch

Foreword

t was a Tuesday morning when I received an email from my daughter's school district informing me that there had been a shooting at a local high school and the gunman had not yet been found. An hour later, the news reported that police had apprehended the perpetrator—a ninth grade student. Two children were left dead and a teacher was severely wounded. Gratefully, my daughter did not attend that school but, sadly, other children and parents were not as lucky.

Having just moved back to the United States after 26 years in Europe, our family has had a lot to adjust to. Gun violence in Europe is a rare occurrence. When I first got involved in teaching CORE Success I had been incensed at the aggression, fairly poor social skills, and lack of good will among youth in Germany. The fact that blatant violence now happens on a seemingly regular basis here in my home country, the United States, has not only shocked me but has turned my teaching into a burning desire to inspire and help turn the tide. The grave and epidemic development of freely expressed anger and violence among our youth, and in our culture in general, is not only unnecessary, it is inexcusable. But the tide can be turned, and that turn starts at home—within yourself—the only place where you have the most control to make a powerful impact.

The journey to my own CORE Success came as a mother fraught with past challenges I'd thought I had successfully put to bed. As a child I staggered under my own mother's distrust of people, including me, and the anger, violence, and horror my father had brought back with him from the Vietnam War. Although my parents were well intending, both verbal and physical aggression ruled in our home and I grew up with immobilizing fear, a sense of isolation, and extremely low self-esteem. I spent decades learning and working on healing with the goal of creating a healthy and happy self. It was not an easy path.

Years later when I gave birth to our first child, Dominik, I looked at that head of jet-black hair and pouchy soft cheeks and knew the gods had shined upon me. He was perfect, gentle, and sweet with luminous eyes and the tiniest little toes. And there I was, absolutely sure that I was going to be the perfect parent. I knew just how I would raise him, how I would discipline and deal with his temper tantrums, how I would magically dissolve all of his fears, his outbursts, and crying fits. I knew, without a doubt, that I would never parent him as I had been parented. I would never make those mistakes.

Well, he'd barely taken his first steps when the fantasy of my parental perfection took its final breath. Through his infant neediness and his toddler clinginess, in all of his small-person glory, Dominik helped me to painfully realize I had zero to few skills to deal with his emerging little self, and I often felt overwhelmed.

In all fairness to myself, though, how could I have had positive, connected, and healthy parenting skills? Where would I have learned them? I'd invested so much time and energy over the years to my own emotional healing and to healthy functioning in relationships and in the world. I'd learned a lot about ownership, self-love, and living an intentional and happy life. However, I had not learned how to joyfully and successfully guide a child on his own healthy and happy journey into personhood. Sadly, that was quite beyond my growth curve when I really needed it most.

In reality, the only parental training I'd received had been as the child of my own parents. We are trained to be parents by the job our own parents do. And, although my parents certainly did their absolute best given their history and abilities, I did not want to walk their path nor parent from their frame of mind.

Recognizing my inability to parent positively was a hard pill for me to swallow, especially since I wanted so much to be the most connected, respectful, and truly happy parent I could be. So I dug into educating myself on parenting's best practices—reading books, attending lectures, and training sessions on self-help, parenting, and spirituality. From practicing non-judgment to gaining certifications as a mediator, group facilitator, and business and life coach, I set my life on a very positive trajectory of self-respect with a genuine commitment to understanding others.

My son became my teacher and I was a willing, albeit sometimes remedial, student. But I made it. I re-created myself as a connected, happy, and peaceful parent, or more accurately as a connected, happy, and peaceful *person* at the most fundamental level. And it had *so* been worth all the effort. The results were evident in my children: empowered and confident, they flourished within our partnership of peace and connection.

Fast forward years later when I stepped back into a classroom to teach, after years of having been an at-home mom. I felt overwhelmed with the new classroom challenges. The Internet and smart phones were the least of my problems. Lack of respect, low self-esteem, aggression, poor communication skills, and a predominantly negative attitude seemed to reign. None of the kids seemed to care about learning, even some teachers at times.

After my initial shock, I knew I had to do something for these kids I was teaching. So, I found in Canada a proactive life skills program for the classroom that had all the components I wanted. I contacted and then consequently collaborated and trained with Shirley Everett, the program's founder. Shirley is an educator, mother, and passionate humanitarian from Nova Scotia and she agreed to come to Germany to teach. Together, we designed and delivered to educators and students in Europe a powerfully effective, compassionate, empowering, and transformational training program: *Learning Peace (Frieden lernen)* (the precursor to CORE Success).

The program teaches adults and kids how to live a positive, peaceful, dynamic life, individually and within a group. The media acclaim we received brought a leading German publisher to our door asking us to write a book and to teach our program nationwide to their educators and students. And so we did. *Learning Peace–The Guide to a Positive School Climate (Frieden lernen® – Das Handbuch für ein positives Schulklima)* was published, I was accredited by the Department of Education, and the German trainings were launched. For years we helped teachers transform their classrooms, hallways, and playgrounds making teaching and learning more effective and more enjoyable for the entire community.

With the success of the educator's training program, we were inundated with requests from parents asking for help in dealing with their own challenges at home. So, I took that work, Learning Peace for Educators, revamped it, added to, deepened, and expanded it into a powerful program for businesses and individuals: CORE Success (www.CoreSuccess.com). I then focused it on the home and created CORE Success for Parents, which I have been teaching internationally now for over a decade. The stories of relationships that heal, of family dynamics transformed, and of parents and kids finally finding ease and having real fun together inspire me. It's my joy to enable adults and youth to build a solid sense of self-worth, and to transform their relationships, their families, and their schools into more connected, supportive, and highly enjoyable experiences. My work is a joy!

My son called me recently from college, a rare event in itself for a college kid! "You're a great mom," he said. Hmmm, silence on my part. I'm rarely speechless, but I was then. I thought he was pulling my leg! "No, I'm serious. I've just been spending time with other kids and their families. It's so different! I can see how supportive and respectful your way of raising us has been. It's made such a huge difference in my life. You're pretty amazing. Thank you." No joke, he said that! Could one ask for a better confirmation?

It is my absolute conviction that we can, in a very real way, change the direction in which our world is racing caused by too many people acting out the deep pain, unbridled anger, or simple confusion they hold inside. We can connect families and empower children in a very real way that will improve life for every generation that follows. It is my vision that more and more parents will discover, commit to, and learn CORE Success at home. It is also my intention that parents will find hope, inspiration, and practical tools here. Above all it is my wish that you, fellow parents, will integrate into your life the tools and concepts that create well-being and healthy connecting with those you love and with others in your world. I believe that together we will, slowly but surely, shift the trajectory we are traveling on—one child, one parent, one family at a time. I hope this work supports you as you create your own unique experience of CORE Success.

May you be well and happy!

Leeza Carlone Steindorf
Portland, Oregon
November 2015

CHAPTER 1

Home Is a Haven

*The greatest gift a parent can give a child is the ability
to become independently happy. And the greatest gift a
child can give a parent is exercising that ability.*

MIKE DOOLEY @TUT.COM

Imagine it's Saturday morning and, after a long work week and seemingly endless struggles, you're off work and able to leave the kids at home
for a while—a short respite from the chaos, complaining, and friction.
You're off on your own. Yay! Your destination? The grocery store.

Standing in the produce section you gratefully realize that you,
alone, will decide what will be served for lunch today. You needn't
haggle about what, if any, chips or sweets will be purchased. You
even get the chance to chat with the clerk behind the cheese
counter without being interrupted. Ah, the joys of shopping
without the kids.

Behind you a lively bunch of people approach the apples. It's a
family and you find yourself slowly retreating from the all-too-familiar

scene. You wanted some peace this morning, thank you. You notice, however, that the dynamic in their family seems different, somehow, from what you're used to. You stand at the display of oranges and observe the scene, discreetly. They speak calmly and are friendly with one another. The parents give the kids tasks— items to find in the store. And, to your amazement, the kids agree, and take off down the aisle on their own. Odd . . . No arguments, no resistance. There's an ease amongst them . . . so interesting.

After you've gotten what you came for, you head for the cashier and the same family happens to line up behind you. Again, they are polite to each other and to you. Their laughter is sincere. The kids start a conversation with another customer. Without being asked to, the little girl picks up some chewing gum, which had been knocked onto the floor.

Outside you find yourself looking for these people and see the family packing the trunk of their car with their groceries. From other items in their car it looks like they're on their way to a picnic or an outing. Your curiosity gets the better of you and you decide to go and ask the parents what exactly it is they have done with, or to, their children to get them to behave, well, so nicely. The parents assure you that their kids are normal and do argue at times, but that they have been practicing CORE Success in their home with amazing results. They add that it is mostly their own attitude and behavior as parents that brought about the most significant changes with their children and in their family as a whole.

On the drive home you make a decision to take a turn in the path you and your family have been on. Feeling ease with one another, having a truly happy attitude, and effective problem solving—that's what you want, too. Now, you just need to find the right vehicle to get you all there. That's where CORE Success for Parents—Clarity. Ownership. Resolution. Excellence—comes in. Here is where you'll find the tools, insights, and concrete help to create the family and home life you've always wanted.

I Was a Perfect Parent . . . Until I Had Kids

I was an expert at identifying exactly what other parents were doing wrong, how their children's issues could easily be resolved, and I had all the answers. Or, so I thought. After having my first child, reality set in, and it must be said: I was an unhappy and harried mother. I did not feel at ease with, or helpful to, my kids. My discipline too often felt harsh and was definitely inconsistent. My love was immense, that was an absolute. And, yet, the challenges of being a parent way too often overshadowed my truly great feelings about being a mom. Fact was, I did not know how to be a good parent according to my own value system, and I was not having fun. It was more than frustrating.

You know how it goes . . . We meet someone and fall in love. It can't get better than this, we think. Soon you are blessed with a little soul, soft and innocent. As parents, we stumble through the initial challenges of infancy, learning vast amounts about things we never before had conceived of. Then comes the first steps, the first words, new horizons to be explored as our child begins to toddle. Our challenges as parents shift. Night-time feedings and colic give way to securing the household chemicals from little hands as we navigate the day with a toddler.

Naturally, we ourselves were parented. However, the skills, knowledge, and tools we need every day to teach, support, and love our children in a way that serves them, and us, is an art most of us did not learn along the way. We fall back on the strategies our parents used on us, some good, some not so great, but generally they were assimilated instead of consciously chosen. Those famous last words, "I will never be like my mother/father," come back to haunt us as we execute the very behaviors we may have found difficult to face when we were the children and they were the parents.

CORE Success for Parents

Over the years now it has become clear that the results of using this program is connected parents and empowered kids. *Connected Parent, Empowered Child* brings to you a program, which is comprehensive, universally applicable (it's been taught successfully in over 30 cultures), and delivers truly solid results. In my search for the common concepts embedded in the entire program and its tools, I arrived at the overarching concept of CORE Success. There are two reasons for this name...

First, each of us has at our core goodness, intrinsic knowing, and the desire to help others. It is the place from which we connect with and empower ourselves and others. At our core we possess, already, all that we need in order to excel at our own version of success. We do not need to add anything, change our essence, or take anything away. By acknowledging that core, we put ourselves in the starting blocks of an amazing journey, the one to ourselves.

Second, there are four main and unifying themes that thread their way through all of my work, through all work of any high value, and those are Clarity, Ownership, Resolution, and Excellence: CORE.

Clarity is the courage to see the truth of what is in front of you, or what you want, transparently and in its entirety.

Ownership means taking honest stock of what is, accepting your part and investment in it, and taking full responsibility solely for yourself and your actions.

Resolution is the committed and consistent seeking of peaceable and fair solutions to dilemmas, or conflicts between people, groups, and their apparently diverging interests.

Excellence is radically living from your highest standard of integrity and ability, knowing the best in yourself and others, and taking all your action from that stance.

The threads of these CORE factors build the foundation and weave themselves throughout CORE Success. At the end of each chapter, you will find a table organizing the elements in that segment into categories of these CORE Success factors.

The intention I hold when teaching trainings and in sharing this book align with the goals of *CORE Success* for parents:

- Empower and equip parents to be gentle yet honest students of themselves and to be kind yet firm teachers for their children.
- Teach each child clarity of mind, good communication skills, self-love, self-discipline, and effective conflict resolution skills. Remind each individual that they, alone, create their experience by the meaning they give to events that take place—their perceptions have power.

- Impart concepts and skills to cultivate and practice self-acceptance, understanding of others, authenticity, and connected relationships. Promote at home the intangible qualities of caring, belonging, loyalty, trust, integrity, and happiness. Develop cohesiveness and positive collaboration in the family unit.
- Enhance the well-being of all family members.
- Encourage and celebrate the unique individuality of each family member.
- Inspire parents to live their personal excellence and employ an attitude of possibility and gratefulness, so as to inspire their children to do the same.
- Facilitate parents to connect from their heart with their kids and empower them to be the best they can be.

What's Practical about CORE Success?

Success is the expression of who you are and how you live. It is not something you achieve.

Understanding that we all live together on this planet, each person in his/her own way and with a broad variety of differences, is one of the main focuses of peace education. Who we are and how we live our lives defines our success. CORE Success empowers the individual and positively influences groups in accepting one's own strengths and weaknesses, developing empathy, being positive, training effective communication skills, learning conflict resolution and problem solving, defining and integrating human values, and consistently practicing cooperative group dynamics wherever one is—at home, on the playing field, in the classroom, and at work – to name just a few.

Teaching CORE Success does not stop when kids grow up, get their high school diploma, or leave home. CORE Success enables one to groom excellence, experience self-satisfaction, and build strong and healthy relationships throughout life. Learning these tools, traits, and ideas at a young age and in a consistent social setting, such as the family and at school, offers the best chance for truly integrating the lessons learned. And, like learning anything, it is a process. It is a long-term commitment that requires consistent training, just like learning a musical instrument or a sport.

When first exposed to something new, an activity or skill, one goes through stages of the learning process—something like this:

- Exposing and observing, perhaps the very first encounter with the subject.
- Experimenting, trying it out, seeing how it works.
- Training and practicing, learning from mistakes.
- Internalizing what has been learned, integrating it into one's life.
- Mastery and ease of application of what has been learned.

For example, when a child first learns to ride a bike, that child has seen people riding bikes, has ridden with a parent, or may be riding for the very first time with his/her own bike.

Next is testing it out: the child tries riding. Naturally, mom and dad get their share of exercise in this phase, where the first few meters are ridden, the first wobbles and woes experienced. The child is told to pedal, look ahead, and hold onto the handlebars ... all at the same time! After a while, the child begins experimenting alone, checking balance, and seeing what happens when a curve is taken too quickly or that stick on the ground is not avoided. Then comes the training part, when what has been learned is refined and integrated into the experience of riding. The pedaling comes easier, the turning more accurate, the sticks either purposefully avoided or taken on as challenges. And, finally, it's smooth riding without training wheels and with the ease and sureness of one who knows. The center of gravity is felt automatically, without mental concentration. Bike riding has been mastered and is now a skill that can bring pleasure and transportation, at will. Another key learning process has taken place.

CORE Success has a similar learning curve. Here you will be introduced to tools and steps for experimentation. Integrating the tools easily will be the natural outcome when you and your family practice over time.

Then, when the tools and concepts have been integrated into daily life, you no longer struggle with conscious effort but act out of habit and/or conviction. You notice that your core, who you naturally are, *is* your success.

What's CORE Success and Why Learn It?

When love and skill work together, expect a masterpiece.

JOHN RUSKIN

Core: The central or most important part of something, in particular the part that is central to its existence or character.

Success: The accomplishment of an aim or purpose (Oxford University Press, 1997).

We are taught to believe that success comes by way of achieving something tangible, something outside of ourselves. I'm offering you a different, more empowering, viewpoint. If we are willing to clearly see and to take ownership of our own core, find our value and our purpose there, our success is not an effort at all. It becomes, then, a logical and inevitable outcome of living from that place of love and excellence already in existence within yourself. That is core success.

All behavior is learned. If positive behavior and effective skills are desired, they must be taught and practiced. Learning and grooming Clarity, Ownership, Resolution, and personal Excellence can only benefit us and our young ones if we engage them on a daily basis. Our world today does little to model or impart self-esteem, a peaceful way of living with one another, fair conflict resolution, or excellence and ethics. The media and, now, life itself seem to dictate that the easiest path is preferable, and that an oppositional stance and aggressive behavior are what's called for. That is a shortsighted and ineffective (not to mention unpleasant) way to go about dealing with the ups, downs, and all of life's experiences.

Every family environment directly, or indirectly, sets the framework for the following markers:

- How you see and value yourself
- How you treat yourself and each other
- How you encounter and welcome new people into your life
- How you deal with persons of authority
- How you communicate
- How you approach and solve problems
- How you deal with conflict

- How you express your emotions
- How you handle mistakes
- The way you celebrate successes
- How you view and manage time
- How you deal with failure
- Your sense of self
- Your sense of humor

Actively teaching positive guiding principles, such as those presented here, is necessary if we want our children to grow up with values and strength of character and as happy, responsible, and independent individuals. Living from your values enables parents to connect with and empower their children. Teaching CORE Success must be made a priority in raising and educating our children. Home is the first place where this step can be taken; *the family is the first, and most important, training ground.*

Home as a Haven

Learning CORE Success at home requires a commitment and takes a positive, proactive approach to all of the markers mentioned above. Equating clarity of mind and ownership, good communication, effective conflict resolution skills, and personal excellence to a peaceful existence is not a stretch but is rather a logical result. If you hone these skills and practice an empowering attitude, then a sense of peace, ease, and comfort is the natural state of being. It is the intentional and consistent application of these tools and principles to our daily events that develops our attitude, self-esteem, behavior, and ability to deal well and positively with difficulties. CORE Success happens when family members make a conscious commitment to living well with themselves and with each other.

Challenges at Home Today	Challenging Results
Low sense of self-worth and self-doubt	Sadness, depression, self-harming, bullying others
Scarce family time, tight schedules	Harried interactions, disconnected relationships, lack of excellence
"Not my problem" attitude	Parent burn out, kids tune out, sense of isolation
High media and electronic device consumption	Social, psychological, and emotional health issues
Lack of understanding, communication	Distance instead of connection
Inconsistent or underdeveloped problem- solving and discipline strategies	Non-cohesive family unit, lack of ownership and responsibility
Pressure to conform	Lack of unique identity, feeling of not being OK
Displayed aggression	Physical and emotional harm, depression, aggression, and power learned as control tools
Complaining trumping gratefulness	Sadness, dissatisfaction, hopelessness

CORE Success Factors at Home	Powerful Results
Self-confidence and the experience of personal uniqueness and value	Self-empowerment, high sense of self worth
Planned family time, easy downtime	Fun, connected relationships, a sense of belonging
Cooperation and accountability	Motivation, a sense of trust and team spirit
Monitored, and balanced, use of media and IT	Educated choices, responsibility, healthy habits
Effective, respectful, and connected communication	Sincere understanding, healthy relationships, sense of safety
Intentional and consistent discipline and trained problem solving	Well practiced life and social, strong conflict resolution skills, dependability
Clear rules and consequences	Trained self-discipline, ownership
Attitude of gratefulness	Happiness, expressed appreciation
Awareness and acceptance of different ways of thinking, being, and acting	Tolerance, celebration of differences, high self-esteem
Fair and peaceful conflict resolution	Ease, feeling safe and secure in oneself and in the world

Why Practice CORE Success at Home?

Sometimes parents say that teachers should do more to help direct and support the personal development of your kids. Often teachers say that it is not their responsibility to teach and train social skills to their students but that it's the job of the parents and the private sector. Who's responsible for what is not in discussion here. The fact is that you, as parents, have a vital role in creating the framework in which your children learn how to trust and value themselves, how to relate to others, and how to see and experience the world.

Our world is changing ever faster and becoming smaller and more connected in many ways. Yet personal connection and authentic interaction seems often to be lacking in our age of technology. Mass media, overexposure to violent and/or explicit adult content, contradictory watered-down morals and values, the deterioration of family structures, and reduced spiritual influence are some factors that contribute to ever more frequent and grave personal, behavioral, and social difficulties in general.

Ownership, responsibility, and self-respect seem to be in contradiction to the definition of freedom our youth is spoon-fed daily, encouraging them to "do what you want, when and where you want, no matter the consequences." At the very least, healthy and responsible action is neither being taught, nor modeled, on any large scale, public, or consistent manner for our youth. Actually, if we look around we'll find just the opposite is true.

What does any parent want for their kids? We want them to be healthy, happy, and well-adjusted people who face a bright and safe future. Our country invests billions of dollars and immense human capacity on security and the military. We are finally giving mandatory attention to the climate change our globe is experiencing. And we are addressing the drastic health issues our culture is facing. We do pay attention when we want to.

But what is being invested in our youth? What serious and focused effort is being made in government, in schools, at home, to effectively and permanently repair the broken system our kids are growing up in? What is being done to teach them a solid and long-term practice of (self) respect, responsibility, and human values?

To help them be empowered in their world? There are private institutions and individual initiatives that are effective, useful, and necessary, but that is not enough. That is vastly too little for the massive mess we are in. This is a social issue that affects all of us and, sadly, only gets national attention when a trigger is pulled and lives are lost. The education and stewardship of our youth is, must be, the utmost priority of this country, of any country. And, we are not doing our job.

Date rape, toxic drugs, self-harming, and plagiarism are just a few of the issues our teens face every day. The media's message that these young kids have to look sleek, sexy, and flawless is a feat no one can manage.

These influences clearly have a daunting effect on everyone. However, for young people, who are forming their self-worth and their view of the world, the impact of these issues is magnified exponentially. It is important to remember that each person who believes that they can make a difference in the world really does. So, you must begin with yourself first. As parents this rule keenly applies. It may be necessary for you to create new beliefs and behaviors for yourself in order to alter your course with your kids or strive toward new goals. This book offers you tools, guidelines, and, hopefully, the incentive to do just that.

The fact is that you, as a parent, have a vital role in creating the framework in which your children learn how to trust and value themselves, how to relate to others, and how to see and experience the world.

Creating a peaceful, connected, and successful family does not happen overnight or simply because you wish for it. It comes from a clear intention and from the dedication of parents to their children. It can be tempting to believe that to engage a family with such a structured program is too stilted and time consuming. Keep in mind, however, that the tension, conflict, and misunderstandings that arise when commitment to a proactive approach is not taken is

> *The fact is that you, as a parent, have a vital role in creating the framework in which your children learn how to trust and value themselves, how to relate to others, and how to see and experience the world.*

vastly more time consuming—and incredibly more stressful. The time and energy invested in learning and applying the principles offered here will provide more free time, more pleasant time, and more loving time together than if it were not embarked upon and the family just moved along as most do.

A home of CORE Success is created through vision, work, acceptance, patience, and love. It is not simply chance that some homes seem warmer, some families happier, and some kids more successful than others. There is a conscious choice, and one well worth making, to create a place where each person feels safe, accepted, and respected, and where your children learn to deal positively with themselves and the world in which they live. Isn't that why you got into this parenting job to begin with? When you come from this place of alignment with your desires and values, you empower your children to create a more positive world and a much brighter future for themselves, and for everybody else.

Keys to CORE Success

⚔ The desire to learn CORE elements as a family is key to successfully implementing this concept. Willingness and a commitment to living well with yourself, and with each other must come first.

⚔ The external forces that families are facing today are powerful. Families need strong tools to navigate troubled waters. Use what you learn.

⚔ Keep your home a place of safety, support, laughter, and love, for everyone.

⚔ Clarity, ownership, resolution, and excellence are the cornerstones of your success as a family. CORE Success is something you live. It is who you are.

ANCHOR WITH ACTIVITIES

Each and every day you are teaching your children. The more consciously you do this, the more effective you will be in imparting the lessons you want your children to learn and take with them into their future. I offer a few activities at the end of each chapter to help anchor the concepts. If you'd like more activities, you'll find plenty of them in the *CORE Success Activity Guide for Parents*. Practicing with these activities may seem odd to do with your kids (being that they are more structured activities that teach something), yet they are set up to be user friendly for any parent who wants to create changes that will take permanent root in their family.

Although the language and framework of these activities are targeted for children up to about age 12, the language can easily be altered, or the content adjusted, to fit the needs of kids through high school. Clients have confirmed that the content is very useful when dealing with the challenges and desires of adolescents in their complex lives. Working in the family, or together with friends, pairing older and younger children for certain activities, also works very well. The needs of your children and those of your family will help determine how you will use these activities.

Note: Many of the activities in this book, and in the *CORE Success Activity Guide for Parents*, call for using a CORE Success Notebook. This is a personal notebook that each family member uses to track their personal thoughts and experiences as they move through the CORE Success process. You can utilize a family craft time to design such a notebook. Be sure to let the kids know why they'll need this notebook and then join them in creating and designing your own CORE Success Notebook.

Harnessing Hope

What's the point?

To assist you, as the parent, in identifying and addressing areas of interest and excitement, as well as possible reservations or concerns in regard to using CORE Success for Parents.

What do I need?

Paper, pencil (and a few quiet moments)

What do I do?

Begin by acknowledging yourself. Write a list, using concrete examples, of how you already are investing energy and commitment daily into supporting the well-being of your family. You've chosen to apply your experience, creativity, and love in an exciting direction with CORE Success.

As with any new undertaking, there may be a mixture of enthusiasm, hope, ideas, and reservations. Use the following questions to explore what may be present for you as you dive into CORE Success.

Personal

- What convictions do you hold about success, attitude, self-esteem, and/or conflict expertise and/or personal excellence?
- Why is this the approach you would like to work with?
- Which of the chapters do you feel most comfortable with? Why?
- Which of the chapters seem most foreign or challenging to you? Why?
- In which areas of this concept do you feel less confident? Which areas would you be tempted to avoid?
- What are your personal goals for this program?

Family

- Why do you feel that your family would profit from starting CORE Success (give specific examples)?
- How do you think working with this program will affect the individual family members, including you?
- What skills will you draw from to assure you and your family will gain the most benefit from implementing this program?
- What role do you see yourself taking in this process?
- What challenges do you foresee and in what areas?
- How can your convictions support you in facing those challenges?

Take it a step further

- Coming from your can-do attitude, what is the best way to get started?
- What comments and reservations does your internal resister (the part of you that resists, avoids, and is skeptical) hold about your plan?
- Fold a paper in half left to right. Write a short dialogue taking place between your can-do attitude (on the left) and your internal resister (on the right). Allow each side to have a say about your intended plans with CORE Success.
- On the back of the paper, have your can-do attitude contemplate and write viable solutions and alternatives to the reservations and concerns expressed by your inner resister.

CHAPTER 2

Connect and Empower

The framework and individual parts of CORE Success® are interwoven, interdependent as well as independent—they are not sequentially linked. That means that you can begin with any one of them first or with all of them simultaneously. The content of each stands on its own in its entirety and comprehensiveness. Since the modules have common and sometimes overlapping content, each one is an optimal adjunct and support to the others. Although the tools of each segment can be practiced and learned individually, applying a few of them at the same time is most beneficial.

Relationships are challenging because each person has their unique desires, history, and behaviors. When these clash, conflict arises. From a pedagogical aspect, conflict and aggressive behavior can be traced back to two general motivational causes: (1) insisting on one's own will or self-serving impulses, and (2) fear-based aggression. It follows then, that training our youth to be competent in the following areas is what's called for to help them be happy, well-functioning, kind, and successful people:

- Self-control, experience of self, empathy for others, and
- Self-awareness, self-confidence, and strengthening of the self. (Winkel, Petermann, & Petermann, 2006)

CORE Success covers these areas and more in depth, offering comprehensive social mastery and the building of strong character.

The Five Keys to Raising Happy, Confident, Responsible Kids

Following are the keys that comprise CORE Success for Parents. The elements of Clarity, Ownership, Resolution, and Excellence are woven throughout each of those keys in this book and in the CORE Success for Parents online training program (www. CoreSuccess.com). At the end of each chapter there are two or three activities to do with your children as a family event. In the *CORE Success Activity Guide for Parents* you will find many more activities to deepen and expand your family's understanding and practice of these concepts and skills.

The five keys, titled as chapters, are presented in the order in which I teach them, beginning with what is usually called soft skills of human interaction and attitude. Since those concepts and skills are fundamental to the following segments on communication and conflict resolution, I teach them, and have written them, in this order. Having said that, each section is comprehensive and complete in itself and may, of course, be learned in any order you choose.

Living to Thrive

The first module is about teaching children to create their own sense of well-being and joy, how to live well together, and to develop self-studentship and a personal sense of responsibility in society. These are lessons in human values necessary to help children live in peace and harmony with themselves and one another. Topics include home environment, gratitude, kindness, respect, understanding and acceptance of each other's differences, happiness, friendship, and team spirit. These lessons empower young people to believe in themselves and the world they live in. By working with this material they come to believe in their importance and to see the fact that they are a powerful influence in bringing about changes for good in their own lives, in their community, and in the world at large. Children will accept their power to change things for the better.

Raising Self-Esteem

A person's level of self-esteem is a major factor in shaping one's destiny. The value children see in themselves is a key factor in determining how well children will thrive at home, at school, and in the world in which they live. Helping to build a positive self-concept and high self-esteem is crucial for the overall well-being, and in the education, of every child. This is the foundation on which everything else is built. This chapter presents practical, easy to implement concepts and steps to nurture the self-esteem of every child and to actively esteem one another.

Resolving Conflict

In recent years there is overwhelming evidence that you are living in an increasingly violent society with a disturbing number of the violent crimes being committed by young people. You must teach your children that violence is neither acceptable nor necessary. You cannot avoid conflict, yet you absolutely can deal with it effectively. Children must be taught the attitude and skills they need to resolve conflict peacefully and with mutual respect. Children must learn pro-social skills and strategies to reduce impulsive and aggressive behavior. This chapter provides ideas and strategies in building understanding, in interpersonal positive problem solving/conflict resolution, effective communication tools, behavioral skills, and anger management.

Discipline with Dignity

Children need a safe, happy, and supportive living and learning environment. How you create your home and its framework helps children to become responsible and learn to behave respectfully. Developing respect, following rules and structures, as well as building and fine-tuning self-discipline are fundamental. This chapter redefines some common concepts to develop cooperative behavior and presents techniques that build effective discipline while preserving the dignity of both the adult and the child.

Abolishing Bullying

Bullying is the springboard for most recurrent violent acts. It is a serious problem with devastating results. Daily reports of violence, suicides, and shootings are proof that the problem is worldwide and worsening. But those are the sensational cases, the ones that make the news, when there are millions of people, young and old, that suffer every day from bullying. The problem is also not a new one, and there are bullies in every walk of life, at all ages, and in all social settings such as school, work, and clubs. Teaching skills at home of how to deal with bullying will prepare children for such encounters and even help prevent it from happening. Practical ideas and useful strategies to help children develop pro-social skills, extend awareness of bullying, and prevent and deal with bullying behaviors are presented in this chapter.

CORE Success for Parents is Unique

This program is extraordinary in the field of personal empowerment, personal development, conflict resolution, and violence prevention, because:

- CORE Success for Parents is a proactive concept. It is based on the conviction, and experience, that giving children the skills, training, and support to consistently practice personal excellence, respectful behavior, and problem-solving skills will develop their natural inclination to live more happily with themselves and with one another.
- This program addresses aggression before it has the chance to develop into violence. It creates an environment where violence is identified as unnecessary. The focus is on creating and training a positive outlook, self-esteem, communication, conflict resolution skills, connection, trust, and safety, thereby promoting the well-being of all.
- By learning all facets of CORE Success for Parents, children learn that success is a way of being and it comes from their

innermost self. They actively learn empathy and emotional intelligence, increase self-esteem, manage anger, develop communication skills, identify values, train inner discipline, acquire conflict resolution skills, express appreciation, express aggression in a healthy manner, master team work, and experience a sense of belonging.

• Focusing on radical acceptance of the person while respectfully correcting the behavior is based firmly in a nonjudgmental framework. That means educating values and desired behavior instead of seeking blame and imposing punishment.

Core Success Tools for You

Self-Studentship

Although the ideas and tools here stand on their own, there's a fundamental precept for using and benefiting optimally from what you will learn here, and that is the concept of self-studentship. When you study a book on cooking, for example, ingredients, cooking procedures, and meals are the content of your study. What we have found to be most useful in making this program pop with success is becoming a student of yourself. That's right—you make yourself the content of your own study, how you think, how you operate, what bothers or delights you. No worries, it's not as hard as it sounds and it's hugely satisfying. Here's an easy acronym to guide you through changing those actions and thoughts you'd like to change: SOADA. See. Own. Accept. Decide. Act.

See – Open your eyes and look at what's in front of you, how you feel about it, your part in creating it.

Own – Take it on, acknowledge it, as it is. Own it by being factual—it helps.

Accept – If you can't accept the event, or the other person, at the very least do accept yourself. (Acceptance does not mean agreement.)

Decide – Set an intention, make a decision to change something, about your actions or yourself, not them!

Act – Move on that intention. Put your decision into action.

Using the SOADA steps of self-studentship as the foundation for this program will greatly increase your success and your sense of satisfaction.

CORE Success for Parents is...

- **Not Prescriptive**. We will not tell you how you should do something according to specific guidelines. Instead, this program allows you to find the way most suitable for you and your family. It also affords you the opportunity to grow into the program and allow the program to grow with you and your family's needs.
- **Not Religious or Dogmatic**. We offer a comprehensive approach to living universal human values—principles that have been taught through the ages and by all major spiritual traditions. Learning and practically applying these values offers people the chance to grow into compassionate, alert, balanced, and happy individuals.
- **Not a Quick Fix**. *CORE Success for Parents* is a commitment that will require ongoing work and dedication. It is a process that is dynamic and far reaching. There is no final product, but the process just keeps getting better! Lessons taught and every action taken is another step on the road to a happier and more peaceful existence. Committing yourself and your family to this process offers deep and substantial results for each person and for the family as a whole.

Keys to CORE Success

- The common desire to learn CORE Success as a family is paramount to the implementation of this concept. This willingness must come first.
- Build on what is already working. Look for all the good! There's a lot of it there. Adapt the concept to work with your family's unique needs and lifestyle.
- CORE Success is something you live. It is who you are.

Challenges and FAQs

- Parents often ask how to fit one more thing into their already fully packed day. It's not a question of *if*, but rather a matter of *how*. Learning CORE Success is a priority. When children are in a safe, peaceful climate, they are happy and positive and are able to live more fully and learn more, and more easily. Make the commit-ment, learn the material, and you will find ways to integrate it. In the end, you'll have much more time for fun!

Build on what is already working. Look for all the good! There's a lot of it there.

✓ When considering if the effort of learning CORE Success makes sense for your family, you may want to consider the benefits, which include: improved home atmosphere, improved relationships with the children and among the children, improved relationships among other family members, less stress, more quiet, and more enjoyment out of your days at home.

✓ How can you turn around a situation where aggression, harshness, disregard, and lack of respect seem to reign? You alone possess the power to make changes in how you deal with yourself and with every person you encounter. That power can, and does, profoundly change you, your relation-ships, and group dynamics. In other words, start in the only place you can... with yourself. (See activity in Chapter 1, Harnessing Hope.)

ANCHOR WITH ACTIVITIES

You Are a Vital Piece of the Puzzle

What's the point?

To show that each one of you has a part to play in promoting a home of CORE Success.

What do I need?

Chart paper, white banner paper, scissors, pencils/crayons/markers, tape or glue, story "The Weight of a Snow Flake" (see Appendix)

What do I do?

Discuss with the children that you all have an important part to play in making your home a safe, caring, and peaceful one. Ask one of your children, or read aloud yourself, "The Weight of the Snow Flake." Discuss the meaning of this story.

Brainstorm ways that each person can contribute to the CORE Success and well-being in the family. Have children write what they themselves are going to do to promote peace.

Draw the banner paper into jigsaw puzzle pieces. (You will need as many pieces as you have family members.) Mark an X at the top of each piece, so children will know which side is the top and front, and then cut them out.

Distribute the pieces and have each family member (including you) draw a self-portrait on their piece. Portraits should be colorful. (Other materials may be used, e.g., construction paper, yarn, fabric, buttons, etc.) Colorfully designed backgrounds add to the overall effect of this project. Your attitude sets the tone, so if you enjoy drawing your portrait, it can create a fun atmosphere for the others! On the bottom of the portrait piece each person writes one word that shares what they have decided is their part to play in promoting a peaceful home—such as, laughter, cooperation, helpfulness. Tape the pieces of the puzzle together or glue them onto another large piece of banner paper. The puzzle can be displayed prominently in the home, maybe with a title as a reminder saying, You Are All a Piece of the Puzzle.

Take it a step further

- Discuss how you can specifically put your decisions to work contributing to positive actions on an ongoing basis.
- Discuss how doing this activity elsewhere could promote a positive and peaceful climate, such as at school, on a sports team, in a club . . .

Note

Discuss with the children how important each member in any group is to the overall well- being and performance of the group—whether it's the family, a sports team, the band, at school, etc. Give the example of the keys on a typewriter or on a computer keyboard. If the letter e is not working and comes up as an x each time, can you imagine what you would end up with? All the othxr kxys function wxll, but this onx kxy not working makxs all thx diffxrxncx. This is thx samx in our family. Xach pxrson is kxy to thx group achixving succxss.

Have the family think about other comparisons to show the importance of each person on any kind of team.

Making It Happen Together

What's the point?

To develop awareness that "together you can do more."

What do I need?

Chart paper, pencils/markers, index cards, photograph of geese, story "Sense of a Goose" (see Appendix)

What do I do?

Find and show a picture of geese. Ask children what they think they are going to learn about the geese. Read the story "Sense of Goose" to the family. Ask the children to write down one word, phrase, or sentence (younger children can give their idea verbally) that comes to mind after listening to the story. Discuss their responses.

- As a family, answer the following questions in relation to the story:
- What does this story have to do with us?
- What can you learn from the geese?
- Give examples of how you can work together to make your family and home more peaceful.
- Will you get more accomplished together? Why is that?

Take it a step further

Ask the children if they know what a pledge is. Discuss with the children the Pledge of an Enthusiastic Team (see Appendix). Invite your children to begin the journey with you to a home of CORE Success: of Clarity. Ownership. Resolution. Excellence. Discuss what that means, and what their parts will be.

Note

Decide as a group where in the house to put the picture of the geese so it will serve as a reminder to always work together. As you continue your journey on the road to a peaceful home, you are making small steps toward creating positive change and peace in the world.

CHAPTER 3

Living to Thrive

Sam is in his early 20s and recently shared with me a very exciting discovery he'd made for himself. He said he'd realized that up until then he had never really lived his life. He always felt at the mercy of events and, as a result, carried with him a nagging sense of dissatisfaction about himself and the world. *When were things going to happen*? *When would life start*? he thought. Sam was so excited in telling me that he had grasped, finally, that life didn't "happen" to him.

He *made* his life happen! And he's now started living his life instead of having his life live him! Sam was thrilled. You could see him full of power and positive faith. What an amazing insight, and what an intentional way of living. How empowering! Imagine getting that concept so early in one's life. That's what *Living to Thrive* is all about, it is weaving the fabric of your CORE Success.

The Core Point ... and Your Gain

This chapter of CORE Success shares ideas, tools, and activities that will help you, and your children, design an attitude that will make your life so much more fun to live and allow you to thrive in ways you haven't until now.

The principles and ideas set forth in *Living to Thrive* need to be taught at home. You need to consciously live by the ideals, values, and principles that you believe in because your children will emulate you—sooner or later. Parents are the most important role models. Remember, children are like sponges. They will soak up the good and the bad of what you do and say. Your actions and words do not go unnoticed.

The concepts in *Living to Thrive* are based on the premise that your worldview is learned and your perceptions are chosen based on your worldview. It is not what happens to you, but how you view what happens and what thoughts you choose to hold that create your experiences.

The ultimate goal of *CORE Success for Parents* is to help you promote a peaceful and dynamic home life where your children can develop their full potential, where they can be happy, healthy, strong, and safe. *Living to Thrive* lays out the factors that help you cultivate that kind of home.

Choice as Your Seat of Power

Happiness is a choice.

BARRY NEIL KAUFMAN

Your life is full of activity, quiet, dreams, responsibilities, joys, and challenges. With practiced awareness you can, to a great extent, direct the course of your life, navigating difficult situations and creating positive ones. More often than not, however, your days consist of what happens *to* you and how you view and respond to what happens *to* you.

Most will agree that it is not what happens in life that determines your happiness, but rather how you view, or respond to, what happens that creates your happiness.

That is a simple yet profound idea. Think about it a moment. In every minute, literally, you have the choice of how you are going to respond to whatever is happening. If someone interrupts you reading right now, or the electricity goes out, or you receive a telemarketing phone call, your experience of that event lies solely in your own hands. You can get frustrated, be open and interested, ignore it all, go for a walk, or choose to use the interruption as a desired break and have a cup of tea. It is not the interruption, the electrical outage, or the phone call that decides how you feel and what you do. You alone decide that.

It is not what happens in life that determines your happiness, but rather how you view, and respond to, what happens that creates your happiness.

In order to have a life of joy, beauty, well-being, and good relations, it is sensible to cultivate and regularly practice skills that empower your choices and remind you that you can intentionally create the life you most want to live.

> *It is not what happens in life that determines your happiness, but rather how you view, and respond to, what happens that creates your happiness.*

Living to Thrive presents ideas and hones skills that will help you define your own CORE Success and live a life that you experience as worthwhile and good. Practicing the principles presented here can lead to dramatic changes. Taking one aspect, and living it deeply and consistently, or taking all of them and applying them daily will have positive effects.

The components of *Living to Thrive* explored in this chapter are: *Attitude and the Home Environment, Gratitude, Happiness, Laughter, Kindness, Respect, Understanding and Acceptance of Differences, Friendship,* and *Team Spirit.*

Living to Thrive teaches young people to define their values. It teaches them how to make choices that serve them best, no matter what events life serves up. Young people can learn types of behavior that will help them to develop the success at their core, to experience their own personal power and goodness, and to live well and in harmony with themselves and with one another.

Cultivate and regularly practice skills that empower your choices and remind you that you can intentionally create the life you most want to live.

Attitude and the Home Environment

Laying the groundwork for CORE Success in the home will lead to connected relationships, a more peaceful family life, and equip your children to be safe and happy and to deal well with the world at large. The world we adults are now creating is our heritage to our children. Supporting them to create CORE Success at the microcosmic level (in themselves and at home) will contribute to a more positive future for them on the macro level of society at large.

As parents you are the role models. You literally teach through your own actions how to be comfortable, aware, caring, and understanding. You also teach frustration, anger, judgment, and unhappiness. Your children look up to you, quote you, and they learn impeccably from how you, yourselves, live and much less from what you preach. You are the one who sets the tone for the day. You do this as soon as you wake up in the morning. If you are smiling, from the inside out, which is not always easy, and greet each other with kindness and a positive attitude, it will have a profound effect on the rest of your day, and your child's day. If a child's day has begun smoothly, it will carry on into her day at school and thereafter. Alternately, if a child's gotten up on the "wrong side of the bed," a warm, friendly, caring parent can help to turn that around as well.

> Cultivate and regularly practice skills that empower your choices and remind you that you can intentionally create the life you most want to live.

Your attitude is the chosen manner in which you see the world and the spirit with which you respond to it. It is a trait that you glean from the world around you. It can, with conscious attention, be retrained to be positive and powerful and practiced at will. If you have not yet designed a great attitude for yourself, you can start now. The attitude you carry with you into your own day, into your lives, contributes greatly to your children's attitudes and the environment in your home.

Life doesn't ask you what you want, although that would be nice; it gives you what it has to offer. Life provides events and interactions and you say, "Oh, look at that." You, through your attitude, are the creator of what happens *after* the event. You choose, "Hmm, I think I want this," or, "I definitely do not want that."

Life gives you the clay but it is your task to form it. If you give your children a lump of clay to mould, the first thing they do is take it in their hands. They feel the coldness, the moisture, the firmness of it, and smell the scent of damp earth. Awareness of, appreciation for, the qualities of the clay itself is the first step. Usually this step of awareness goes unnoticed in daily life; awareness is, however, vital to the process of moulding the clay, of living your life. Otherwise the clay, like life, is taken for granted and remains just a clump.

We suggest making that initial step of awareness conscious. The first step in creating a life you enjoy, then, is appreciating what you are given each day as a gift and, like the clay, it did not come from you. However, you, alone, have the complete freedom to live and use that day as you wish.

Firstly being aware, and then being grateful, you can mould and shape the events of your life as you choose to live a life you desire and can enjoy. As we know, many days we're offered events that feel like hurdles at best. Even then we can seek the good and be grateful for the small gifts in and around those hurdles. It is important to help children realize that they have the power to see and enjoy every day as a gift. It is a choice. You choose to live it to the fullest, or let it end without finding its fullest value for yourself. Your attitude decides.

Television, the Media, and Screen Time

A number of years ago, my husband returned unexpectedly in the middle of the night from a business trip. Wanting to be quiet and not wake me, he kept the lights off as he moved around. Lying in bed, I was sure there was a burglar in the house and something horrible was about to happen. I was close to hysteria as he bumped around in the dark.

That event, and the bone chilling terror I felt, was a turning point for me. Later, I realized it wasn't the situation that was so terrifying, but rather it was the ingrained pictures in my mind from years of watching on the screen all the gruesome things that could happen. I swore to myself from then on I would never have that kind of fear again. So I decided to only watch positive shows, not one more movie or TV show where someone is tortured, murdered, raped, or in which there was blood spilling, a human being hunted, or evil figures lurking in the dark.

And, so, after about a year of watching talk shows or inane comedies. I simply stopped watching TV altogether. The more I engaged in other activities, the more I found media to be dissatisfying stimulus. I now get my news from select sources. I read more, sew more, jog more. Best of all, I'm now totally relaxed, even when unexpected or off-the-wall events take place. My default is no longer fear.

Our kids have been raised without TV (yes, very uncool of me). We watch carefully chosen films and movie time is a family event, not something to do on your own because you are bored. The kids have spent most of their free time doing sports, outside in the woods, playing games, or at the library. It demanded more of us in our parenting role, and we had to swim upstream often, but their healthy development was more than worth that effort.

Today, almost adults, my kids watch movies, are steeped in the media, and are plugged into the Internet with the best of them. So, what's the difference? Why did we go to all of the effort and resistance to reduce, or even eliminate, TV and video game intake from our family's "living" room? Well, they use media as a choice and not as a default. They know life without a screen in front of their faces and are very discerning in what they watch.

Let me be clear: I am not suggesting you or your family quit TV. However, a majority of my clients have found a reduction in media consumption to be a positive transformation for their family. What I am urging you to do is to be an informed media consumer and diligently intentional about what you feed your mind and, especially, what you allow the media to feed your child's mind.

The powerful impact of the media is something you can observe daily. Here is why, specifically, media has such a detrimental effect on your personal, and on your family's, well-being.

In the best case scenario, television and electronics (computers, tablets, smart phones) are used as tools to inform, educate, and at times communicate in written form. Children like the action, the stories, and the ability to interact immediately with a medium over which they have personal power and input. In addition, it keeps them occupied, which some parents want. You will not be able to completely eliminate media as it has become woven into the fabric of modern life. However, there is much you can do to inform yourself and be clearly intentional with media usage.

Certainly there are times that using media to educate, inform, and even entertain is very desirable. I am not speaking about the healthy use of media here. What I am addressing is using media to occupy, babysit, offer companionship, or making our TV set or computer an intimate member of the family. That may sound absurd, but it is unfortunately more reality than not.

Your family will profit from reducing media to a backseat role in your family life. Your family's mental well-being and having more time to be a tight-knit, relaxed family are only two good reasons to make a change. Here are some other reasons why extensive TV/media consumption can be highly destructive:

- Due to prolonged viewing of an electronic screen, a child's eyes can suffer fatigue, blurred vision, headaches, dry eyes, and eye strain (Kozeis, 2009).
- The media feeds us a constant diet of violence and aggression. This, then, becomes the norm. Between the years 1937 and 1999, 100 percent of all animated feature films contained violence. In 21 percent of 33 of the most popular video games violence against women is portrayed (Council on Communications and Media, 2009).
- The message content of many, if not most, TV shows, computer games, apps, etc. is to sell us a world perspective of "us against them." You are programmed to believe there is a negative force intentionally out to get you, and that the most powerful and aggressive one wins in the face of that pervasive threat.
- By age 18, the average American child will have viewed about 200,000 acts of violence on television alone (Council on Communications and Media, 2009). Consistent media

consumption of this kind creates the conviction of a malevolent world, and of the need to be wary and to hone aggressive behaviors. Even our dreams are impacted by negative media content.

- An inordinate amount of your day, hence your life, is dedicated to the "activity" of media consumption. The average child today aged 8–18 spends 6 hours and 21 minutes *per day* using entertainment media (Council on Communications and Media, 2009). From your approximate 16 waking hours you spend at least half of that at school or work. Hence, with another 6 hours spent on media, your time for family interaction is vastly reduced.

- Limited eye activity and inhibited neurological firing while watching a screen for a longer period of time leads to various physical results, such as, eye discomfort and sight impairment, physical restlessness and hyperactivity, and a systematically trained short attention span.

- Watching TV literally rewires the brain of an infant according to studies done by Dr. Dimitri Christakis at the Child Health Institute at the University of Washington in Seattle. ADHD symptoms have been proven to have a direct relationship to childhood TV viewing (Christakis, 2009).

- Research on autism has found a link between the underlying genetic predisposition to the disorder and the early exposure to TV viewing (Waldman, Nicholson, & Adilov, 2006).

- Shortly after beginning to watch TV, the brain changes from beta waves (alert brain activity) to alpha waves (hypnotic waves) where areas of the brain for critical judgment are bypassed (Kubey & Csikszentmihalyi, 2003). This is crucial given the high rate of TV violence and sexuality. Your child's brain is being regularly trained in a passive state to accept this information!

- Media consumption detaches viewers from "real life" and plugs them into a virtual reality. Especially through computer games, children learn that they have ultimate control over events and conditions. This, of course, is unrealistic. As a result, children become less able to deal effectively and comfortably with the daily interactions of their real lives, where they obviously do not have such omnipotent control.

- For optimal brain development, children need physical activity such as climbing trees, jumping, doing cartwheels, and even falling down. The reduction of physical activity (in the outdoors especially) of an entire generation of our youth due to the inactivity of high media consumption leads to less stimulation of the body and, hence, the brain.

- The personal ability to create stories and images—in short, to develop an imagination, to fantasize—is less developed in children with high media consumption. This ability is essential in problem solving, to extrapolate information, and in making mental connections.

The message here is to be an informed and intentional consumer of media. Choose the media sources and monitor what your children are consuming. Awareness in this area is vital for your child's health and well-being. Thankfully, there are now many Internet sites that offer educational as well as adventurous and value-based content for kids. Do your research on the Internet for games and films, adding to the word "games" in your search the addition of key words such as: values, educational, peaceful, nonviolent, social skills, social issues, kindness, emotional intelligence, self-control, self-esteem, conflict resolution, and similar; and to "films" the search words: family, children, value-based, wholesome, nonviolent, and similar.

"Keep your thoughts positive because your
thoughts become your words.
Keep your words positive because your words become your behavior.
Keep your behavior positive because your
behavior becomes your habits.
Keep your habits positive because your habits become your values.
Keep your values positive because your values become your destiny."
MOHANDAS 'MAHATMA' GANDHI

Core Success Tools for You

Television, the Media, and Screen Time

Wow. So, given the pervasive presence of media in your lives, what can you do? Be intentional and be smart:

- When viewing TV and permitting video games, adopt Smart Usage Rules:

- Limit time on media.

- Watch the show or play the game before your child does. You may be very surprised.

- Make choices with your kids before they watch, or play.

- Stay informed of their content. Being nosy in this regard is part of being a responsible parent.

- Control Internet access and use parent controls for permissible content (especially on your child's computer).

Tips to make TV or movie time a special event, instead of a daily diet:

- Make popcorn or offer treats for the show that the kids usually aren't allowed.

- Purchase a home projector and use a blank wall as a screen so it feels like a real "event."

- Let the kids choose the movies. They definitely know what is acceptable.

- If your kids are different ages and/or both sexes, alternate the choices each time to please everyone.

You cannot easily avoid media in the world today and probably don't want to. But you can do a whole lot to reduce its influence, choose exactly how you want to use media in your lives, and decide what information your kids take in from these sources.

Centering and Stillness

In our world today silence and solitude are rare and im-
mensely precious. When we find them they restore us
to a state of well-being. We feel a sense of harmony and
peace. Spiritual nourishment, creative insight and a con-
nection with everything that exists become possible.

EILEEN CAMPBELL

There is no doubt that the world has become incredibly fast paced. As adults, you feel the effects of time pressure, deadlines, and the speed of everything from emails to the seldom and almost extinct art of conversing. Children, being still more connected to their natural biorhythms, are strongly and adversely affected by the fast pace and stress around them. Many illnesses and disorders in today's children are being effectively treated with relaxation and centering exercises, or mindfulness practices as they are often called, such as yoga, somatic education, progressive muscle relaxation, and meditation. The reason is that our bodies and minds can take up their normal paced and healthy functioning when returned to a state of quiet and calm and, hence, serve us better.

If you observe small children, their world is timeless (assuming that their physical needs have been met)—whether they are taking a walk, picking up a piece of lint off the floor, or exploring your face with their hands, time is no factor for them. They are completely present and, as a result, simply do not rush. If they are motivated toward something, they surely can go fast, yet there's no sense of haste in their speed. Over time, however, you train out of your children this natural sense of going at one's own pace. You drill them with expressions like: hurry up, don't dawdle, time is of the essence, we'll be late, slowpoke, etc. The phrases, like the pressure, are endless. As soon as they become adjusted to your hectic pace, you begin trying to counter it by telling them to take their time when writing, to chew their meal slowly, and to not drive so fast.

Jean Liedloff wrote about the Yaquana Indians of South America in her excellent book *The Continuum Concept: In*

Search of Happiness Lost (Liedloff, 1986). She had lived with these people for 2 years to study just why it is that they are so extremely peaceful as a culture. The answer, she found, is that their attitude toward, and actions in, raising their young is radically different than ours here in the West. Just one example relating to time: The Yaquana carry their young children, as most indigenous people do. Naturally, however, the young children do walk when they are able to or when they are too large to be carried anymore. When traveling as a group, however, the tribe only travels as fast as the slowest person walking. That means no one is rushed to keep pace; there are no disgruntled adults at not going fast enough. Imagine! The adults travel as fast as the slowest child. A Yaquana child has never experienced the sense of having to rush, keep up, or not being as fully "able" as the adults around. The sense of self-acceptance that stems from that simple act alone is profound.

Wouldn't it be more beneficial to train youth to actually maintain their natural rhythm, inner calm, and sense of connection and timeliness? Developing this depth of self-awareness, of calm, of core knowing, is fundamental to healthy emotional and physical development to a child's health, concentration, sense of well-being, and creativity. Especially for children, it allows for a positive experience of self, something that is detracted from and often destroyed through the use of media. Enabling children to be intimately familiar with their inner world and sense of well-being would benefit not only the children, but you and your family would profit enormously as well.

Stilling can be used to access inner calm, to help both relaxation and concentration at the same time. It involves easy posture and being attentive to your breathing. Stilling is for being with oneself, turning away from what's out there to what's in here. Today's world constantly bombards you with a stream of input in the form of telephone, TV, music, advertising, video clips, DVDs, Internet, smart phones, interactional computer games, and the daily exchange with others. Your senses are consistently overwhelmed and overworked.

Turning within by using different approaches to mindfulness offers you a needed and replenishing opportunity to notice where you are and what is going on inside of you. With all of the input from the outside world, you often lose touch with what you are feeling and what your needs are. In stillness you can turn your senses away from outer stimulation toward the inner workings of yourself. Plus, it's a mini vacation! Practicing stillness, or mindfulness, is a tool that can help you in many ways including lowering your blood pressure, increasing your mental capacity, understanding yourself, and helping you deal more calmly with your family, coworkers, and friends. Indeed, practicing stillness helps you maintain a peaceful state as you go through your day. Stillness can enrich your inner world and offer you the foundation of "inner direction" in your daily life. Being centered within makes most situations easier to deal with. It gives you access to the tools you already possess so you can better deal with the challenges life offers up. In the stillness you can experience a sense of peace and calm from which your goodness stems and can then flow more freely.

"The power for creating a better future is contained in the present moment: You create a good future by creating a good present."

ECKHART TOLLE

Core Success Tools for You

Centering and Stillness

When stress enters your life, here are five simple steps to walk you through stress to centeredness again:

1. Notice that you feel stressed (seriously, this is an important first step!).

2. Feel, and then name, what you are feeling in your body and your mind.

3. Remind yourself that you have a choice in how to respond to the situation; you, alone, are in charge of how you feel at that moment. There is no blame in this, only gentle power.

4. Ask yourself: How do I see this situation as bad for me? (That doesn't mean it is bad. It is neither good nor bad for this purpose. Seeing it as bad for you causes stress and clouds your judgment. It is very useful to crystalize how you believe it is bad for you.)

5. Finally, find a way to see some small gift for you in the situation, despite the appearances. Focus, then, on that gift. Or, find that place inside yourself that is always calm, no matter the circumstances, and take action from that place.

Although these steps sound easy, they are not easy to carry out when the going gets rough. With practice, however, you'll begin to experience a marked difference in how you respond to life's stressful situations.

Grooming Gratitude

. . . the more you become a connoisseur of gratitude, the less you are a victim of resentment, depression, and despair. Gratitude will act as an elixir that will gradually dissolve the hard shell of your ego—your need to possess and control—and transform you into a generous being. The sense of gratitude produces true spiritual alchemy, makes us magnanimous—large souled.

SAM KEEN

Gratitude is a quality of being thankful for what is. It is the willingness to show one's appreciation for kindness or goodness in our lives, and leads to wanting to return it in like kind. It is a characteristic that can be learned and practiced. True abundance begins with gratitude and thankfulness. We have been trained to see what's missing, the glass as half empty. This, unfortunately, leads to many negative effects on our emotions, behavior, and personal interaction. Being thankful, on the other hand, for the goodness that does still exist among all other factors focuses one's attention on the things one does have. Gratitude helps you feel positive, and helps those things to grow in your awareness.

Some ask, "*Why* should I be grateful? What does it get *me?*" Well, other than shifting away from a focus on lack and what is not working, experiencing gratefulness has the unique quality of giving one a sense of delight and wonder about the world. Understanding that you are part of a greater picture eliminates a sense of isolation. Reflection on the whole and its inner workings and connections can lead to awe and an appreciation of how it all works together. Gratefulness leads to feelings of well-being, hence, to happiness.

When things don't go your way, when you have experienced a loss, large or small, it is easy to get lost in the difficulty and apparent misfortune of the event. We are not suggesting to not see what you have lost or has not gone as desired. It is by seeking, exactly among those uncomfortable circumstances, the things that are still good that helps you move through such challenging experiences more easily.

As with all undertakings it is not so much what you do as how you do it. Gratitude is a case in point. Every day from getting up in the morning, taking a shower, eating, going to school or to the office, shopping, working, cleaning, planning, and communicating, there are a variety of events that take place. As humans we categorize, at some level of awareness, each situation as either good or bad for our well-being. If you give it no value, then it usually goes unregistered in your memory of the day. In practicing a gratitude attitude you can learn to view any and all events with an eye geared to creating what you can enjoy—meaning, looking for the gifts inherent in all events.

> In practicing a gratitude attitude you can learn to view any and all events with an eye geared to creating what you can enjoy—meaning, looking for the gifts inherent in all events.

This practice of appreciation brings a number of benefits to you and to those in your life. If we can look at a particular situation and see it in its entirety, you can tone down the emotional charge and allow the gifts it holds for you to seep into your experience. What is called for is practice—turning your eye from that which pops into view automatically (frustrations, disappointments, etc.) to that which is present (goodness, needs met, safety, etc.) yet momentarily outside of your awareness. With this practice, the habitually automatic viewpoint can be re-trained. You will then create a new automatic response that serves to draw out more enjoyment of the events that take place.

For example, how often are you on the road, heading for an important meeting in your car, just to be delayed by road construction? Usually a fist pounded on the steering wheel and a short call on your cell phone takes care of this frustration and inconvenience. And then you move on to the meeting, finally, for which you are late. Upon arrival, you find that some of the papers you had sent never arrived and an important participant was not informed of the meeting at all.

Again, frustration arises that things have not gone as planned or as you had wished. The sequence of events goes on, but the point is clear. Now imagine, instead, the following:

Sitting in the traffic jam, you use the time to appreciate the people out there in the glaring sun or freezing rain working hard to repair the streets so that you can drive at all. You then turn your appreciation to the Earth for offering you her resources to pave roads. This enables you to commute from point A to B quickly and without saddle sores. At the meeting you could express your gratitude to the person who photocopied all the papers that did arrive. Then notice how valuable the person and his input is to you and to your efforts, who unfortunately was not informed and, hence, not present. Be grateful that person is on your team at all.

Here's another example: As a parent you arrive home after trudging through long lines at the grocery store, only to find the kids have used the living room furniture and your expensive wall hanging to build a cave. Your boss and some colleagues are coming for dinner this evening and your spouse is in bed with a migraine. When you see the trail of popcorn leading to the entrance of the cave on your freshly vacuumed carpet, you feel as though you could scream. You may even do so! You would rather turn around, get back into the car, and drive away to a more peaceful environment rather than be confronted with the reality and chaos of what must be done here and now.

Now would be a perfect time to practice a gratitude attitude. You could even do so together with your family, if you were so inclined, using your own experience as the lesson material. Begin with the grocery store where you bought the popcorn. Be grateful that there are stores within your reach literally bursting with any and all foods you could desire, and you even have the money to pay the bill. In observing the popcorn kernels, you can take time to bless the person who invented the vacuum cleaner, which will take care of that in no time. Those kernels are a reminder of the hungry little, or big, mouths of children growing up too darn fast. As for your spouse, remember the times you have been supported and loved when you were down and out. A hug from you could make all the difference in the world to that special person at that moment.

And then come the children. Listen to the noise coming from the cave and watch them in action. Be thankful for that creative energy that is so valuable for our world. Surely their presence in your life, the joy, fun, insight, and wonder they offer daily, is a gift. And as for the cave, crawl on inside and enjoy 5 minutes of smelly kids and burnt popcorn. It will, without a doubt, be the most magical moment of your day. Really, just sit back and enjoy. Hear what excites these young souls and how they see their world. Connection on that level is surely something to be grateful for.

And, then, ask those little souls to be your Speedy Gonzales working buddies in transporting the cave to another room and in doing things to get ready for your special guests.

Although none of the externals have shifted, your perception of them certainly has. You find yourself feeling a deep sense of gratitude for the very simple aspects of life. This then empowers you to deal with the things that challenge you with more vigor. It is a turn of the coin, a slight of the hand, yet a change that can carry far reaching results. Independently of letting others know you are thankful for their efforts, your quality of life is enriched by practicing a sense of gratitude. It just feels good.

Choosing gratitude is not an act of disregarding frustration you may feel. It is, rather, shifting your focus in such a way that frustration gives way to feelings that nurture you and bring you more pleasure in the events that take place. This practice is, at the beginning, not an easy task for you have been well trained in another way of seeing, trained to complain. However, since you are constantly seeking to gain more enjoyment out of your life, practicing an attitude of gratefulness is a powerful exercise, which you alone have control over, and will ultimately get you more of what you want—to feel good.

Your home life is part of your life as a whole. If you practice gratitude within yourself, you personally will profit without a doubt. In practicing with the family, those people you interact with daily, you multiply your own gains from gratefulness by offering your loved ones the chance to do the same.

Core Success Tools for You

Grooming Gratitude

When first waking up in the morning or when taking your morning shower, think about all the things that you are thankful for, such as, waking up, your health, hot water, standing on strong legs, indoor plumbing, your family, your job, the sunshine … try to be both general and specific. This sets the tone for your day. When you go to bed at night, call to mind at least three things that you are specifically grateful for that happened during the day, such as, a successful meeting with an important client, a child made a new friend, and we laughed a lot at dinner tonight.

Turning your focus away from what's wrong and lacking to seeing the goodness and abundance around you is not an easy job. You have not been trained to be grateful for seeming obstacles and disturbances. But you can retrain yourself to concentrate and comment on what is working instead of what is not—to accentuate the positive. Life offers you what it offers you. You alone decide how you will respond. In gratefulness you can watch what you had thought of as mundane or even negative transform before your eyes into gifts of grace. Your heart is warmed, your thoughts uplifted, and your experience of the day is wrapped in the irrefutable feeling of being part of something greater than yourself, something wonderful and good. Practicing a gratitude attitude will strengthen and enrich you in ever widening circles. Practice is what will give you that experience.

Honing Happiness

There is no way to happiness; Happiness is the way.

THE BUDDHA

Happiness is said to be a feeling of joy, contentment, satisfaction, and inner peace. Unfortunately, most people believe it's something only the future can bring or some event can deliver to them. You hear people say, "I will be happy when it's summer; I will be happy when I'm in high school; when I'm in university,

I'll be happy; I will be happy when I get a job, when I get married, when I have children; I will be happy when I retire." If you define your happiness in the future tense, you can never be happy. As John Lennon said, "Life is what happens when you're waiting for life to happen." It is important to help children realize that regardless of what happened this morning or last week, or what will happen later this evening, tomorrow, or next month, now is where happiness is. You carry it within you at all times.

In actuality, the past only exists to the extent your mind recalls it. The future is, literally, an unknown. In fact it is today, this very moment, that comprises the only reality you have. That can either sound sappy, or be seen as a profound truth. A happy person is not a person in a certain set of circumstances—being famous, being wealthy, etc.—but rather a person who chooses a certain attitude. The way we think creates our happiness.

Many people believe that their happiness depends on getting what they want. Happiness is not a product of what you get. Happiness is a choice, your choice.

You can look at the beliefs behind every decision and choice you make. What you want is merely that: something you want. That thing, event, or person does not harbor your happiness. There are no hidden promises of happiness included in fulfilling that desire. For example, imagine you have been pining for a new car and you have finally scraped together enough money to buy it. The color, size, speed, and feel of it are just perfect. As you slide behind the steering wheel, you feel you could not be happier. You seem to be floating. Your desire has been fulfilled. What more could you want? But how long does that sense of happiness last? A week, a month, until the car gets its first scratch, or until you find an even fancier one that you would like to have? It is not getting what you want that makes you happy. For invariably when you do indeed get it your happiness is short-lived. You then focus on the next thing you want. So, where does happiness live?

You have the choice in every moment, and in every situation, about how you are going to see it and respond to it. Whether you get what you want, or you don't, does not have to impinge on your sense of well-being, your feeling of happiness. Try it out. The next time you don't catch that green light, you fail that test, you miss your important appointment, or you don't get acknowledgment for your efforts, realize that you can choose your reaction to the event. Tell yourself that *you alone* choose how you feel about it. You are free to feel a sense of well-being, even when things do not go as you want. This is a sobering, simple, yet liberating practice. Above all, it offers you an empowering opportunity to sit in the driver's seat of your own experience.

How often have you seen it happen? You are with your child and he or she is just as happy as can be until someone offers him or her something tempting—an ice cream cone, a trip to the zoo, an x, y, or z offer—and, for whatever reason, your child is not allowed to have it! Only moments ago your child was totally comfortable and happy. But then the complaining starts, the whining, and stomping of feet, the unbearable truth that your child cannot be happy without having the x, y, or z offer. How immediate the change is from happiness to unhappiness. Is it then really possible that the happiness depends on attaining that thing? Can't be. Imagine if that very child were taught that he could choose to be happy, or maintain his sense of joy, even if he doesn't get what he wants, doesn't get that treat? And imagine if he practiced that way of choosing over time. What an impact that could have on the child's entire life!

It is also observable that happiness is contagious. When I'm feeling happy, I share that joyful energy with all those around me, creating an environment in which it is easier at least for others to also choose to be happy. This is a win–win situation with a compounded effect. When you share your joy with others, you expand it in yourself.

You are the sole creator of your own happiness.

Happiness can only come from within. Even when you do get what you want, it is your take on it that creates your sense of happiness not the object itself that creates it. It is a choice you make about how you want to feel at *any* given time. You are the sole creator of your own happiness.

So it is immensely helpful to make your children aware of what happiness is, that happiness comes from within, that happiness lies in the present, and most importantly that you will experience more happiness by expressing happiness.

A Look at Laughter

The most wasted of all days is one without laughter.
E.E. CUMMINGS

Laughter is not only fun and an expression of happiness, it is indeed cathartic, coming from the Greek word *kathartikos,* meaning to cleanse. It purges, releases, creates movement, and cleanses you. You even change the way you look at the world when you laugh. Recall a time that you were down or something challenging happened. And then, for whatever reason, a good laugh brought you to breathlessness. Didn't the situation then look different to you or you at least felt differently about it? Through laughter you can change your perspective and create a new view. Such a shift can offer us a refreshing experience of happiness.

Laughter is more than the use of one's muscles and voice, it coordinates and has a profound effect on the body's various systems. Recent research shows that 1 minute of genuine laughter leads to deep relaxation in the entire body. The science of psychoneuroimmunology has proven that 30 minutes of humorous activity, laughter, and a happy, positive attitude can, among other things, cause the release of endorphin chemicals into the body—endorphins are your body's natural painkillers (Berk, 2001).

What else does laughter do for us?

- Reduces muscle tension.
- Discharges surplus nervous energy and relaxes the nervous system.
- Invigorates circulation and drops blood pressure to below normal levels after an initial rise during laughter.
- Triggers the release of endorphins, a brain chemical that produces feelings of euphoria and contributes to pain relief.
- Improves oxygen levels in the blood.
- The diaphragm convulses offering a massage to the body's internal organs.
- Facial muscles are given a workout.
- Boosts the immune system.

- Cortisol, a natural anti-inflammatory, is also produced by laughter.
- Nonderogatory laughter connects us to others on a direct, nonverbal level.

Kindling Kindness

Kindness is the language that the deaf
can hear and the blind can see.

MARK TWAIN

Kindness is showing that you genuinely care for others through understanding and by doing helpful and thoughtful deeds.

You cannot assume that children will automatically be kind and caring, especially in a world that can be very unkind, thoughtless, and even cruel. Children are being bombarded with messages that encourage unkindness and even cruelty—at home, in school, among peers, in the media, through music and electronic games, etc. Nurture kindness, compassion, sharing, goodness, and love in children so they will feel good about themselves. Only then can they make a difference and cultivate a life they love and a world in which we can live well.

The way to do this is to help your children understand what kindness means and the importance of expressing their kindness. You want to encourage them to act out their kind thoughts, which brings happiness to themselves as the doers and to the receivers who may respond with their own happiness.

Your actions always pass through you first, being the very first recipients of your treatment of others. This holds true whether you are being kind, angry, complimentary, or aggressive. If one wants to throw dirt or flowers at someone, one must first hold that dirt or flowers in their own clean hand. Your mind, your body, and your heart registers every thought and action that you then act out in your world. Since your quest for personal well-being is what motivates you in life, it would be beneficial for you to choose carefully that which you permit to pass through you and outward to others. Choose your thoughts and actions by asking, "is this going to deepen my experience of well-being, or not?"

Kindness is a case in point. Helping the man next to you in the grocery store, whom you don't even know, by picking up the apples he dropped, brings first to you a sense of being thoughtful and useful. It just feels good to do a kind deed. The next recipient, the man, feels a sense of kindness being passed on to him. This chain will continue on if he, too, chooses to pass it on to another person he encounters.

You offer kindness by being mindful of the person's particular situation and what would be useful to them at the moment. And, showing kindness to others does not necessarily entail more effort. It can be a simple matter of including a new person into a conversation, passing on information to someone who is seeking it, or offering acknowledgment to someone.

Being kind with your words is easy. How often do you see someone wearing a striking blouse or walking with a happy gait? It is quite easy to mention that very fact to the person: "Hey, I like the sweater you're wearing," or, "You sure seem happy today with that great smile." This lets the positive thoughts you have about your world benefit others, expanding your own sense of feeling good. Thus you make more room for other positive thoughts in your inner world and gift others with some goodness to enrich their inner world. Being kind is a win–win situation. The kindness and respect you give multiplies within you automatically.

Kindness doesn't mean that you should let people take advantage of you or that you be indulgent or permissive. In fact many times the kindest thing you can do is to be firm and directly honest with someone out of caring for his or her well-being. For example: Friends don't let friends drive drunk. Kindness shows and grows strength and confidence.

Some examples of kindness are:

- Invite someone else to go first.
- Offer someone else the "biggest piece."
- Just give someone a sincere smile when you feel like barking back.
- Find something admirable to say about someone who is being spoken ill of by others. (It's an automatic gossip-stopper!)
- Listen to your kids' favorite music at dinner time (as loudly as you're able!).

- Ask a new staff member to join your after-work get together.
- While getting your cup of coffee, bring one for your spouse/coworker as well.
- Help your child find that special "cool" shirt they want to wear today.
- Bring an extra piece of cake to work and share it with someone you don't know.
- Take the time to be present and kind to someone who seems to be having a bad day.
- Thank the bus driver before leaving the bus.

Raising Respect

Respect means seeing and valuing the intrinsic worth of a person and treating them with that dignity. This absolutely includes self-respect, by the way! It is based on the Golden Rule: Treat others the way that you want to be treated, or that you know they would like to be treated.

Nurturing respect is essential for self-esteem, develops interpersonal relationships, and helps children to become responsible citizens who value every human being. Respect is vital for success in every area of your life. It is a clear and disturbing trend that today's children are far less respectful toward themselves and others than previous generations. Children have many influences in their lives. Many of these influences are sending messages to our youth that encourage disrespect of oneself and other people. Children are often treated disrespectfully by the people in their lives—parents, relatives, teachers, coaches, peers, etc. If children are to learn how to have respect, they must be treated with respect. This is how behavior is learned and will be emulated.

There are many influences in the world that have a great effect on your children, many of which are not helpful: the decrease of positive role models; the increase in everyday rudeness; the use of harsh, inappropriate, and vulgar language; the normalizing of violence and disrespectful language and behaviors through television, CDs, videos, and computer games; and the public portrayal of females and minorities in a discriminatory light. Since your kids are deluged with these external influences, it reinforces that it is crucial that you actively teach your children the meaning and importance of respect, and that you foster respectful behaviors.

Self-Respect: By taking stock of your strengths and weaknesses, by learning to see that you alone choose your responses to events, and by being aware of your desires and your dreams you come to know yourself, who you are, and how you want to be in the world. Being conscious of the person you are, and living intentionally and congruently according to your personal values and dreams, is the foundation for self-respect. Taking positive action based on this knowledge of yourself is living a life of self-respect. If I believe in the power of the spoken word, I refrain from cussing. If I value health, I eat a good diet and exercise regularly. If I value love, I express my caring for others in tangible ways. You also then avoid or correct situations that would impinge upon or devalue who you are.

When someone does not respect your wishes, you address them in a calm manner and explain what it is that you want and do not want (see Chapter 6, *Resolving Conflict*). You then work toward assuring that your desires get fulfilled, as long as other involved parties are respected as well. If your behavior is not aligned with the values you hold, then you clean up your mess. You take responsibility for your actions by speaking with the parties involved and by making, or offering to make, amends.

Walking the talk of your convictions, you construct and build upon the cornerstones of the respect that you have for yourself and can then offer the same quality of respect to others.

Manners are an outward expression of yourself and your respect. They mean behaving so that you uphold a positive view of yourselves and others, thus contributing positively to your social environment. Behaving in a way that makes you feel good grows out of your own sense of self-respect. Offering your seat on the bus to an elderly person or a pregnant woman, helping up your classmate who fell, and refraining from making fun of others are acts that make all parties feel good. These acts not only show kindness but respect as well, and with practice such deeds form your daily behavior. Over time positive behavior contributes to your sense of worth, which you can then turn around and give back as positive action to others.

Using "thank you" and "please" are not just formalities. They are an expression of how you are feeling about things. To say to someone "thank you very much for helping me solve that problem" helps you confirm your personal gratefulness for the gifts that you receive on a daily basis. It also lets the other person know that their kind deeds are appreciated. That interchange is a valuable confirmation of the principles that we are speaking about in this chapter. Gratefulness should not be confused with the pro forma of saying an absent-minded thank you every time something happens, but rather literally using the situation to express your appreciation, letting other people know that you do appreciate what they have done for you.

Similarly, when you receive a compliment the tendency is often to say, "oh, that's not true," "no, I didn't do that much," or "it wasn't that important." This only negates the acknowledgment the person is offering you and denies you the opportunity of self-acknowledgment. It is beneficial for both when the receiver of the compliment offers a sincere thank you. "Thank you for letting me know you feel that way," or, "Thank you for acknowledging that." Try it; you'll like it!

Saying "please" and "thank you" does become a habit. There is nothing wrong with that, especially if you consider that using cuss words and being rude also becomes habit. If a young person says a bad word every time something goes wrong in their eyes, he or she is literally training the use of language that brings him/her down. Especially today, our youth don't need any help in training negative traits—they get enough training from their environment. You need to help them acquire life-affirming, empowering habits, starting with the use of polite words. And such training can lead to a change of behavior and attitude. In any case it is at least more pleasant for all involved than the trained negative words and habits.

In addition to these daily acts of respect, you can also maintain a sense of self-respect by adhering to norms set forth by our culture. By adhering to these social moirés you show respect for those in your surroundings—whether you know them or not makes no difference. By showing respect for the "agreed upon rules" of the culture, you find yourself living together in more harmony and less friction. For example, saying "excuse me" when belching in public, covering your mouth when you cough or yawn, using a napkin when eating, and holding the door open for someone are all acts of respect for others as fellow human beings. These are behaviors that come from valuing doing good. All parties win when good manners are used.

Practicing manners in no way suggests that every person goes through life mimicking like a puppet. On the contrary, by underlining your self-esteem, also by training behavior that is respectful, you become clearer about who you are, what you believe in, and how you want to live your life. Nothing could contribute to your individuality more than that.

Positive words of encouragement can boost you up when you are down and can let you know you are well thought of. Hearing such words regularly can support your personal sense of well-being. Acknowledgment, when used as a tool for better relations and building self-esteem, lets you feel confirmed, especially after you have invested time and energy into something. Such acknowledgment is holding up a mirror for you in order to view your own accomplishments.

It is important that we encourage others without placing an evaluation or judgment on what the person has done or achieved. The emphasis is placed on the individual's effort, improvement in comparison only to her own past accomplishments, and on the joy of observing the person in action. For example, "It was so much fun for me to watch you run that race! You showed your courage." Or, "It shows great progress that you got a B on this paper when your last three papers had C's. Your effort to improve is really showing! You are doing great." This keeps the receiver's focus on doing one's best according to one's own standards and striving toward self-set goals (see examples below). When you are acknowledged, you can then sit back and observe what you have done with a sense of satisfaction. "Yes, I have worked hard and my efforts have paid off," or, "well, it isn't perfect, but I have improved a lot since last time." Simple statements that specifically observe another's effort, mirror what one sees, or state changes can be powerful words of encouragement. Like the following ...

Core Success Tools for You

Raising Respect

- You've worked all morning without giving up. That is determination.
- You completed that drafting project to the exact specifications your teacher gave you.
- What an imaginative idea. No doubt you will be able to implement it.
- I see that you have given your best on this homework.
- Even though it didn't go as well as you wished, you worked at it diligently and showed your desire to succeed. I believe in you.

Accept Differences, Seek to Understand

All human beings are born free and equal in dignity and rights. Everyone is entitled to those rights and freedoms.

UNITED NATIONS' UNIVERSAL DECLARATION OF HUMAN RIGHTS

If you look around, there are very few people (outside perhaps your small circle of friends and family) who look like you do and who share your personal views, history, and preferences. You interact daily with a myriad of individuals who are different from yourself, not only externally, but internally as well. The differences you see in others—skin or hair color, accent of speech, way of dressing, walking, communicating, eating—can seem odd or even put you off. The reason for that is that it is foreign to you and you often move away from, or may even fear, the unknown. But is it an imperative that the unfamiliar must be shunned or feared?

Widening your scope of vision to include and accept all people, their attitudes, as well as habits that may seem foreign, uncomfortable, or even contrary to your way of living can enrich you tremendously. The willingness to practice acceptance and kindness leads to peaceful coexistence.

Core Success Tools for You

Accept Differences, Seek to Understand

Thankfully, over the eons, we have developed the ability of differentiated thinking. The key to connecting to each other, to being understood by others, and to understanding them is to observe and accept the differences, and to go a step further even and celebrate them. The first step then is to understand the differences. In a new or unusual situation, instead of judging whether it is good, or bad for you, you can ask yourself, "What can I learn from this person or situation?" which can then definitely be seen as "good for me." What in this situation is a useful tool, something you can learn, change, or apply to your own life? If you look at the differences in others from this perspective there is always a lot to learn, especially when an open heart and an open mind are leading the encounter.

Where you grow up, who your parents are and what they do for a living, which language you speak, what food you eat, and the books you read are only some of the things that make you up to be the person you are. Since every person on this planet has a different set of life circumstances under which they grew up, even within one family, it is a given that you will be different from one another. Deciding to understand where another person is at, where someone comes from, and inquiring sincerely as to why someone does what they do can lead to an expansion of your own perspective and deepen your understanding of our world. And, in addition to serving you well, understanding and accepting another person offers them the gift of feeling they belong, just because they are who they are, all differences included.

Judgment vs. Assessment

To be clear, when I speak of judgment in all CORE Success materials, I differentiate between the term "using good judgment" (discernment in thinking, decision making, and making an assessment) as opposed to judging negatively against, and condemning, one's self and others. We use the term judgment here in its meaning of making others wrong or bad under the assumption one is ultimately right or has a position of superiority. Judgment against others is a trait that can be destructive and is a practice often born out of a need to feel better than others, or a need to compensate for a lack of self-esteem. Judgment against others is learned and can be unlearned.

Often making judgments about others is based on lack of information. Here is a poignant example. Early one evening in a busy subway train in New York City a father and his four children entered a full compartment. The children began yelling to one another, throwing things, and acting wild. The tired commuters, on their way home after a long day's work, were less than pleased with their behavior. The father sat quietly staring into the distance, apparently unmoved by the disruption his children were causing. One irate traveler approached the man and asked not too kindly, "Can't you control your children?" The father looked at the woman a moment before responding and said in a quiet voice, "We have just left the mid-town hospital where we lost my wife, their mother. None of us know quite how to deal with it."

No one appreciates being on the receiving end of judgment. It is crucial to one's own well-being, and for the positive bonding of people of all groups, ages, and nationalities, that you begin the process of practicing acceptance and nonjudgment. This becomes feasible when you come from a place of believing that every person is doing the best they can given their current state of understanding and abilities. That doesn't mean you have to agree with what they are doing, but you can accept them as people, nonetheless. If you practice seeing the world from this angle then it becomes much easier to release the pattern of judgment.

Assessment is looking at someone or something and seeing the qualities and attributes without a moral statement about it. I can tell my child that he has left his room messy with clothes on the floor (an assessment) without telling him only dirty people leave their space such a mess (a judgment).

You usually judge others when you don't like the way things are. Take the same example: you do not want your kid's room to be messy and dirty. You do not want to clean it yourself, nor do you want the work of reminding her all the time to clean it up.

That's reasonable. However, the charge you feel when telling her to clean it up usually carries a judgment. The unspoken "How could you?" or ""You still haven't gotten it right!" does not get you the desired result, and even creates more friction around the subject. So, what's there to do?

The neat thing is that in every "I don't want" or "How could you?" lies an inherent "I want." The key is to figure out what that want is and to work toward that want instead of expending energy judging. Finding the "want" eliminates the need for judgment and for the emotional punch you give others when you don't like the situation. By becoming clear about what you want, you can then request it, work toward it, and stay pleasant, yet firm, until things move in that direction.

Core Success Tools for You

Judgment vs. Assessment

You can redirect energy and time spent focusing on and moving away from what you do not want

 **Don't want this!**

and invest it with impact instead into moving toward what you do want:

Definitely want this! → ☺

Your words, the thoughts and pictures in your mind, have tremendous creative power. Take a moment to think about what you really want. You may have to dig a bit, but when you discover it, imagine what you want in full detail, an action, an object, an experience, a vacation, a relationship. Allow yourself to want it, no matter the appearances of the current circumstances. Then decide what action is necessary to move you in the direction of getting what you want. Specifically define and then take those steps and you are actively creating in your life that which you want to have. Even if, in the end, you do not get the exact desired result, you are being proactive and clear about where you want to go. That is a powerful way to live. Plus, it is a lot more fun moving toward a passionate "want" than away from a distasteful "not want."

If I want my child's room to remain fairly clean and for my child to learn the value in keeping himself and his personal (and common) space clean and tidy, then I take action and move in that direction. From that stance, I ask myself, "What will help me get what I want?" Telling my child that he is bad for not cleaning up does not get the desired results (as some of you may have noticed).

Go for what you want by creating a learning environment, go back to basic training: help the child learn to fold his clothes to understand that spiders and other bugs like it when things are not moved for a long time, to recognize that he finds his items more easily when they are put back in the rightful place, and to realize how he feels when entering a tidy room as opposed to a messy one. Give him a time frame and a practical 1, 2, 3 to-do list to get the room clean. It is true, however, that with some kids this last item will take longer to learn. (Believe it or not, though, we've even had success going back to the basics with teenagers!)

Talk the child through these steps and thoughts, slowly and consistently. These steps may be more time intensive at the beginning, but save time and energy in the long run from repetitive scolding and conflictual encounters. Plus you are moving, literally, toward getting what you want: a more tidy room and common space. What you focus on gets bigger. It really is that simple.

Not judging does not mean agreeing with and supporting behaviors or actions that are clearly against your values. Instead, however, turn your attention to improving the circumstances that can be improved rather than concentrating on what others have done wrong. Interestingly enough, you judge in others that which you are judging in yourself. If you don't believe that, take a little test: Recall a recent judgment you had of someone, how lazy the homeless person is, how poorly your partner cooked that meal, how out of shape someone is, etc. Now ask yourself if there is something in that judgment that you judge yourself for.

Core Success Tools for You

Practicing Nonjudgment

The first and most effective step in practicing nonjudgment is to look at and release judgments about yourself. The next time that you are less than satisfied with your own performance or behavior, be aware that you have done your best for where you are at this point in time. Then look concretely at what did not work well and devise a plan to do it differently in the future (again, moving toward what you want). If there is an error that needs to be corrected, or a wound that needs to be healed, then do so.

The next time that you find yourself judging someone else's behavior, appearance, or performance, remember that person, too, is doing his/her best given their current state of understanding and abilities. Remove yourself as the judge. Offer a helping hand, if possible, and look beyond what your perception tells you about the person in front of you. Wonderful things can happen when negative constraints are removed.

You Bet I'm Right!

As parents we all tend to do it: we insist we're right, just because. Well, it's a habit, and one more than worth breaking! Believing your viewpoint is *the* right one, or that you have the market on absolute truth, is a costly affair. You set your relationships on the line when, in actuality, there can be no right or wrong in perspectives. When you take the stance of being right, you actually train your kids out of sharing with you authentically, even when you don't intend to do so.

It behooves you to train an attitude of engaged listening and accepting that your own stance is equal to someone else's, even if they are much younger than you. Facts may be correct or incorrect—the light is on, it is 82 degrees outside, my hair is brown—but stating with conviction that it is way too bright, it's too darn hot, or my hair looks drab are opinions that reflect only a person's take on the observed facts. An opinion neither validates nor changes a fact. An opinion is, however, a person's subjective, and valid, perception of a fact. This differentiation demands a different handling of facts and opinions. You can assess facts as being correct or incorrect. You cannot tell someone their perception of a fact is correct or incorrect. It's their perception and it stands validly as such, even if you don't agree.

Making others wrong when their behavior, beliefs, or opinions conflict with your own, insisting that you are right, is an absolute communication stopper. Self-righteousness limits connection, hinders progress, and, all too often, destroys relationships. In Chapter 6, *Resolving Conflict,* we examine how to share your own opinions in a respectful manner, respectful to yourselves and others, and then listen to others in a way that allows you to truly hear them. This type of connecting is vital to strong and effective communication and to healthy and functioning relationships.

Friendship and Team Spirit

A friend is a gift you give yourself.

It is important for children to also have sources of happiness and laughter outside of the family and children's friendships serve many important developmental functions such as social support, companionship, and practice for future relationships. As early as kindergarten, children who have made friends at the beginning of the school year have more positive perceptions of school and better academic performance (Birch and Ladd, 1990).

Research also shows that friendship plays an important role in both preventing bullying and helping children cope once it has started. Teaching friendship skills is very important and children have to learn these skills. Children need to learn and practice skills that help them make friends—for example, being honest, being loyal, conversing, discovering shared interests, showing appreciation. Children should also be taught how to join a group successfully and how to integrate others. This is very important for successful relationships with their peers. It is also important that children learn and practice how to manage disagreements fairly without harming the relationship. We must realize that these skills need to be taught to children. We cannot assume that they will just develop on their own. Often, if left to chance, children won't develop healthy relationship skills.

Children who don't have friends often have low self-esteem, they feel rejected, they set themselves up to be a target for such things as bullying, and their overall well-being suffers. Therefore, it's very important that we help children to develop positive friendships and connections very early in life. Teaching kids to live happily and well with others helps them know what good friendship means and how to groom those relationships in their lives.

The Power of Teams

Good sportsmanship is reacting to a critical situation in a manner that builds up yourself and your team in a positive way.

HARRY SHEEHY

A team is a group of people gathered together to achieve a common goal. Clearly, then, your family *is* a team and you, as parents, are the team leaders. Your daily activities, as well as outings and family projects, provide a good framework to teach the team skills outlined in this chapter—happiness, kindness, gratitude, nonjudgment, and respect.

Children have an extraordinary amount of energy on all levels. To support children to keep that power flowing in a positive way, it is important for their environment to channel their creative, social, and physical energies in order to address them as whole individuals. The bodily power that children carry with them absolutely needs an outlet. Not only do team sports, family outings, and group recess activities in school direct that energy to flow in a positive manner, thus reducing aggressive tendencies, but the spirit of teamwork can be taught as well.

The qualities that can be developed through consistently participating in family activities or projects and team sports are: a positive work ethic; setting goals; defining and working toward success; the understanding of excellence; the two-sided coin of winning and losing; the spirit of healthy competition; humility; training sportsmanship and character; allowing, developing, and enjoying enthusiasm; and accepting and offering criticism and praise.

In a formal team setting, it is the coach's responsibility to actively focus upon these aspects during all trainings, games, and competitions. As parents, you can also support the development of these traits at every opportunity in your family activities, and encourage your children to be active in healthful events and daily tasks in your family.

The healthy physical and emotional expression of pent up tension, frustration, and aggression that is channeled well in sports and group events—in the family or on formal teams—will greatly support a more peaceful atmosphere at home. Getting the kids involved in a team outside the home goes even a step further by offering children a framework to train values and social skills that they will carry on into their lives, while letting off steam at the same time. The tools learned in a positive team setting are ones used daily later in life in the workplace and in social settings. By making integrity, character, and sportsmanship important lessons for kids to learn, you will develop team spirit at home and all the way around.

Core Success Tools for You

Good Sportsmanship

To facilitate the development of team spirit among children at home, whether playing or working together:

- Make chores and tasks a family project.
- Include some fun family competition while getting work done. Who can rake the most leaves, the kids or the adults? Will the guys or gals be the first ones to get home from the bike ride?

You can anchor the idea of team spirit in the family by asking:

- Was the experience fun?
- What do you remember about the game, project, or activity?
- What could we do next time together?

Turning the emphasis in sports from winning or performance and turning it toward enjoyment and goal setting is of great value.

Conclusion

There's already so much ground covered in this first module, but time is on your side. It's a process. There is no doubt that these principles are not only important, but key to creating a life that is self-gratifying for you and your family. Daily application, awareness, and integration of these ideas will, over time, lead to more fulfillment, less dissatisfaction, and a successful family life. There is no magic formula for being happy or content. There are, though, certain components that have been defined over time, in many cultures and in many settings, that support an individual to get more out of every day, feel better about life in general, and experience core success. *Living to Thrive* offers effective practice in this arena of living life from a positive perspective and with a hopeful heart.

CORE Success Factors of Living to Thrive

CLARITY	OWNERSHIP	RESOLUTION	EXCELLENCE
		Manage TV/media	
	Know percep-	Accept	Practice gratitude
	tion is chosen	differences	Center yourself
Raise awareness	Groom (self)	Practice	Use music
Be kind	respect	nonjudgment	Choose happiness
See the good	Define what	Reduce sibling	Laugh
	you want	rivalry	Focus on friendship
		Stop insisting on	and teams
		being "right"	

Keys to CORE Success

⚔ A positive view of things is acquired through training, just as a negative viewpoint is.

⚔ Every thought creates the words you use. The words you use manifest themselves to create the world you experience. Hence, it is wise to choose your thoughts carefully.

⚔ Your decisions create power.

⚔ Modeling the process of choosing positivity will empower your child to do the same.

⚔ Each person is doing their best at any given moment, according to their current state of understanding.

⚔ By choosing love more consistently than fear, you can change the nature and quality of your relationships.

⚔ Within each person you meet is the seed of a friend. You can choose to help that seed to grow.

⚔ True acceptance is without demands or expectations.

⚔ Your differences are superficial and only carry the meaning you give them. Only the countless ways we are all alike has any importance at all.

⚔ Other people do not have to change in order for you to experience peace of mind.

⚔ Whether you think you can, or you think you can't, you are right.

Challenges and FAQs

✓ *"Why should I teach my children to be kind, help others, and practice respect? They aren't treated that way by others, so why should they then behave that way?"* There is only one answer to this question: Because it feels good. There is no guarantee that you will be treated accordingly. But it is a certainty that by treating yourself and others according to positive values, you will feel better about yourself and your world. In the end, that is all you can do anyway. You can change only your own steps. Change your own steps and the overall dance has to change in response.

✓ *"I've been working so consistently with teaching CORE Success to my children but they're still fighting a lot. What am I doing wrong?"* First, you're not doing anything wrong! Work through all areas of CORE Success for Parents and see what areas need more focus. Look at exactly what you have accomplished. Acknowledge yourself for your effort and your successes. If the situation seems to have stalled, back-track and work on something that you thought was already understood, such as, the need for stillness, respecting others, or understanding differences. Talk about the situation with the family. Together find out where the problem areas are and make a plan of which steps would be best to take next. See the section on Sibling Rivalry in the Chapter 6, *Resolving Conflict*.

✓ *"My environment has a part to play, too. I can't live as though I am not influenced by the world around me."* This is true and you are advised to keep it in mind. Yet living a mindful life, one of joy and purposeful well-being, means to choose with awareness which factors from the world around you want to include in your lives and which factors you want to avoid. You interact with your environment daily, yet it is important to remember that you remain in the driver's seat. You decide in which direction and in what manner you proceed, eventually to get you to where you want to go.

✓ *"Too much positive is unrealistic. Life just isn't like that."* Let's differentiate between looking through rose-colored glasses at a seemingly perfect world and looking to see the positive in life and practicing a gratitude attitude. To "practice a positive attitude" means taking in the events of the day and your experience in relationships while looking for what is working well, taking the gifts that are there, and being grateful for the kindness and goodness inherent in all things. You remain aware of the difficulties, taking note of the conflicts and problems, all the time working in the direction of resolving those difficulties and strengthening relationships that may be faltering. You rise to the challenge with good intentions, believing that others, even though you may not be able to discern it at times, are doing their best as well. Were you to only look through rose-colored glasses, it would mean going through life with blinders on. It would mean not being aware of the difficulties at hand, and, hence, not addressing them in an effective and assertive manner. If you were to expect the world to be perfect, you would set yourselves up for constant disappointment and the necessity to issue blame upon those who have disappointed you. This is clearly not what we are referring to when we speak of an ample positive attitude.

✓ The fear of making mistakes, the fear of feeling humiliated, accounts for the conditioned behavior of blaming. It is the reason that many people never reach their full potential. We hold back from living so as not to feel we have failed. It's your job, as an adult, to challenge yourself to look at your own fears of making mistakes. It is your job to overcome those fears so that the children in your life can overcome their own, or avoid developing such fears.

✓ When you make so called mistakes, being willing to admit them and to clean up your mess is essential to the learning process. Admitting that you do not know something, especially as parents, allows young people the freedom to not have to know everything either. It is very liberating to not have to know. Removing this pressure often opens the door to true curiosity and the desire to learn about those very things you do not know about. Not knowing ignites growth. The next time in a conversation about a rather well known subject that is, nonetheless, foreign to you, try just saying, "I don't know very much about that. What exactly is that about?" Or, the next time that you make a blunder own it, embrace it, and admit it in front of everyone present if appropriate (in my case with a sausage shooting off my plate at a fine restaurant while fellow diners applauded). Most likely the atmosphere will loosen up and you will receive acceptance for your humanness and openness. (The waiter graciously picked up the sausage and thanked me for providing his dog with a treat for its evening meal!)

You do not have to be perfect, even as a parent. Your kids are your greatest teachers. And when you make mistakes, admit them to yourself, and to others, and love yourself a bit more for your imperfection.

✓ If some of the exercises or lessons don't feel comfortable to you yet, because you have not yet internalized these ideas, try them on anyway. The best way to learn something is to teach it. Go through the lessons with your kids. Do the exercises alongside them. Listen to your inner skeptic and question its validity. Make it an experiment and see where it takes you.

✓ You do not have to be perfect, even as a parent. Your kids are your greatest teachers. And when you make mistakes, admit them to yourself, and to others, and love yourself a bit more for your imperfection.

ANCHOR WITH ACTIVITIES

Our Family's Mission is ...

What's the point?

To help the family gain awareness of their purpose as a family, to add understanding the usefulness of a mission statement, and to create a personalized mission statement for the family. To create individual mission statements.

What do I need?

Writing paper, index cards, CORE Success Notebook, pencils/crayons/markers, samples of mission statements (see below)

What do I do?

Discuss what a mission statement is: A mission statement defines the direction, intention, and spirit that a group or individual has as its motivating force. A mission statement is the vision that calls us forth to do our best, to grow into our potential, and provides the focus for individuals to work together in a way that will create a magnificent whole.

Then show examples of mission statements. Discuss how a mission statement is like the definition for a word. It defines you, your values, and makes a statement to the world about who you are, what you do, and why. There are three questions that a mission statement answers:

- What is your purpose?
- What is your intention, or what do you want to achieve?
- How will you do this?

It is stated in the present tense, is short, and clear.

List the values and characteristics that your family find important: growing, laughing, serving others, helping, loving, having fun, learning, including others, etc. Write down the responses. Then have each person write a short mission statement for the family on an index card answering the three questions above.

Collect the index cards and summarize the points on paper, combining similar points and discussing different ones. Together, write a family mission statement that is agreed upon by all. When you've got it down, write it out and post it in the home so all can see.

Examples of Family Mission Statements

We all work to create a peaceful and happy home where everyone is respected, encouraged to learn, to have fun, and feels safe and loved. We all contribute to a home where we can share and not be put down. Each of us does our personal best to fulfill our dreams and help others fulfill theirs.

The mission of our family is for all of us to participate and believe in ourselves. We cooperate and help each other. We are kind, respectful, and have fun together. We do this by doing our best and by telling ourselves that we can do it!

Examples of Children's Mission Statements

My mission is to be all that I can be by listening, participating, helping, seeing, and believing (10 year old).

To dream! Every human being deserves to dream and create ideas. I will dream extraordinary things and follow them (11 year old).

I am nice and good. There's only one of me, so I'm important (5 year old).

Take it a step further

Have each person make a list of what they value and what they would like in their personal mission statement. Then discuss these ideas as a family. Each person then writes their own personal mission statement in their CORE Success Notebook. (It's a good idea to have a CORE Success Notebook as a diary for each family member.) Post the mission statements, if desired, and refer to them when things get tough or people could use a reminder of what their intention is to live by.

Revisit the mission statements periodically, especially the family one as kids grow, to see if it's still on point, or if it needs to be changed.

Family Meeting

What's the point?

An opportunity for each person, and especially children, to share their thoughts, ideas, opinions, and feelings about many issues: things that are going well, things that can be improved, new ideas, personal and family successes, responsibilities that need to be addressed, personal concerns, and general sharing. The family meeting provides an equal opportunity for each child to contribute to decision making and problem solving, and to learn about being a family. It gives them the tools, and format, to become effective problem solvers and contribute to family team building.

What do I need?

Writing paper and pencil; chairs in a circle; popcorn?

The family meeting may be formal or informal, simple or complex (depending on your family's style). Sitting in a circle as a family helps bring everyone together and helps kids see themselves as equal to everyone else in the family. Choose what items will be shared and alternate the topics. If you all are discussing a problem, use the talking stick to find creative solutions and agree on how to carry it out. Take some notes so you can review the progress, concerns, and successes at the next family meeting. You can meet weekly, biweekly, or monthly, again depending on your family's desires and schedule. A regular meeting is highly suggested.

It is important to have each person feel ownership of what goes on in his or her home. The family meeting helps children to feel valued, gives them a sense of belonging, and helps them realize that each person is vital in promoting a successful family and a peaceful environment.

What do I do?

Here are some guidelines in setting up a family meeting, which may be useful to you. Tailor the following depending on your family style, time frame, and age of kids:

- Explain to the family the intention of the meetings (to offer a space for each person to share and to be heard; to have time together as a family; to have fun; to work out any current challenges; to plan and dream).
- Decide together what kind of format would be desirable for your meetings, such as, beginning with a game, drawing, singing, using the talking stick, before a family outing, closing with a song, prayer, making the meeting a fun family event.
- Stick to that format, more or less, so a reliable pattern emerges.
- Have a clearly defined beginning and ending ritual for the

meeting, such as, a song, a hug, holding hands. This will offer a clear intention for the meeting and help any issues that are being discussed have a starting and ending point.

- Set regular times, scheduled on the family calendar, and keep them.
- Decide on the time frame for each particular meeting and stick to it, so the meetings will be something to look forward to, rather than a disturbance in family life.
- Include in the meeting a time for each person to have free space to share. Remind everyone at the beginning of the sharing that nonjudgment, no interrupting, and complete attention is desired.
- Use an object for the speaker to hold while speaking, such as, a rock, crystal, talking stick. Using an object reminds the group to pay attention to the speaker, who may talk without interruptions, questions, or objections. Each person will have a chance to speak, so everyone can relax and listen to the speaker. (See activity Talking Stick Untangler in Chapter 6, *Resolving Conflict.*) Help smaller children bridge their shorter attention span by having drawing or quiet play items available.
- Take notes, maybe in your own CORE Success Notebook, that can be referred to at the next meeting, to establish whether expressed wishes, difficulties, or questions have been addressed between meetings.

Letters of Thankfulness

What's the point?

To help children see the varied and numerous things in their lives for which they can be grateful.

What do I need?

CORE Success Notebook or paper, pencils

What do I do?

Discuss that there are many things that we experience, use, and see daily that we take for granted, but that are really gifts to us. Have the children come up with some examples like the car, clothing, air, and sunshine. Then have each person list the letters of the alphabet on the left hand side of a page in their notebook or on paper, one letter directly under the other, one per line. Explain that next to each letter they are going to write one thing, beginning with that letter, for which they are grateful. For example, on the line with "T," one child wrote "tooth brush" and explained that if someone had not invented the toothbrush, we would all have a ton of cavities!

Then everyone fills in their letters with words that start with those letters. They do not need to go in order and may jump around the alphabet. However, they should fill in all 26 letters. Younger children can be paired with older ones or with a parent. When done, discuss how the children felt about the exercise. Pick some letters of the alphabet and ask the kids to share and explain some of their responses.

Variation: At the end of the allotted time period, there may be some empty lines for some people. Ask everyone to switch papers or notebooks. Each person will then fill in the empty lines with items for which they themselves are grateful. This exchange will lead to reading through the lists and to fun questioning of one another. For example: "Why are you grateful for a broom?" Answer: "Because I can always retrieve my ball off the garage using the broom handle."

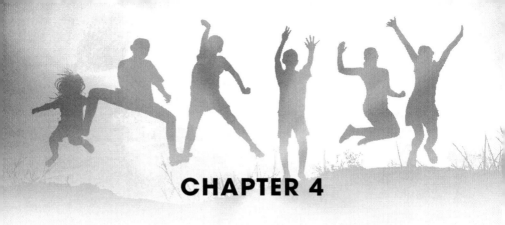

CHAPTER 4

Raising Self-Esteem

Whatever you can do, or dream you can—begin it.
Boldness has genius, power and magic in it.
JOHANN WOLFGANG VON GOETHE

E very day so many people hide who they truly are. As infants we have an intact sense of worth. We have had no reason to doubt it. Over the years your self-worth gets dented and bruised and we often feel that we are not quite as good as we could or should be. Sometimes these doubts take place in our inner silence; sometimes they spill over to the outside world. Take for example our youth in their formative years who often hide behind their appearance. Young people often believe that by looking and dressing a certain way they will be cool, accepted, and respected. They believe being thin, beautiful, wearing spiked hair, or sporting Nike shoes is their entrance into the club of being valuable. Then I will be worthy, they think. But self-esteem goes much deeper than how you look or whether you are keeping up with the latest trends.

The Core Point ... and Your Gain

Self-esteem is an individual's personal evaluation of one's own worth as a human being. It indicates to what extent one considers oneself to be capable, important, successful, and valuable. Self-esteem results from the quality of relationships between a child and the messages received from the significant other persons in that child's life.

Having healthy self-esteem means a comprehensive and balanced view of and acceptance of self, knowing and embracing both strengths and weaknesses. We are not speaking about being boastful or arrogant. Boasting stems from an unbalanced and negative view of self (yes, negative!) blown into extreme proportions as a false front and form of self-defense. Although it seems paradoxical, boastful and arrogant people suffer from low self-esteem. They then try to compensate for it by proclaiming their worth to all who can hear in an attempt to claim it as truth for themselves.

The other extreme is never admitting success or a job well done. Always denying or playing down the things you do well. Don't do it! You are withholding acknowledgment and praise from yourself, as well as from others.

Believing in yourself, knowing that you are capable of achieving your goals, and accepting your weaknesses gives you the impetus to be grounded, fair, and positive in your dealings with yourself and with others.

Building and strengthening self-esteem is a broad subject. The focus here is on aspects that contribute to a healthy sense of self: self-concept/self-image, self-esteem, creating and using a positive attitude, the erroneousness of "mistakes," getting to know feelings, the role of acknowledgment, the power of the spoken word, listening, and self-esteem builders.

Concept of Self

Your **self-image** is built through a variety of factors such as physical abilities; self-observation and comparison; your appearance; language abilities; verbal feedback from family, friends, and peers; and social integration and interaction (how others react to you). **Self-worth** is how valuable you see and feel yourself to be. It is an inner sense of your own worth in the world and is created mainly through your relationship with yourself. **Self-esteem** is how valuable you feel you are to others and to the world at large. It is built and maintained in direct connection with others—parents, siblings, friends, students and teachers, and later partner and coworkers. It arises from how you believe to be valued by others.

How they treat you and what the quality of the relationships are that you have with them create, bit by bit, what you believe your value to be—to them, to yourself, and ultimately to the world in general. Self-worth and self-esteem are interwoven and interdependent. This crucial matrix of self-image, self-worth, and self-esteem has long lasting effects not only on how you value yourself, but also how you then value others, behave toward yourself and others, as well as greatly influencing what power you have and what direction you believe you can take in life.

Dr. Carl Rogers, renowned as the father of humanistic psychologist and person-centered therapy, established that our concept of self begins in early childhood and is heavily influenced by our parents (Rogers, 1977). For this reason, it is paramount that as parents you pay close attention to raising and maintaining a healthy concept of self in your children.

Self-Esteem

Self-worth supersedes all else. It is living the permission, the freedom, and the right to be who and how one really is.

To hold persons in esteem is to hold them in high regard, to appreciate them and their worth. Learning to love yourself completely teaches you how to love others. Seeing and embracing your true nature—accepting the flaws, strengths, dreams, and fears—that make up who you are, allows you the generosity to understand others. They have different weaknesses and strengths than your own, but they have them just the same. There is no necessity to put on a good face, or try to be different or better than just how you are. By doing so, you can also accept others just as they are. This is not permission to act inconsiderately, thinking only of yourself and causing havoc when you find yourself in a stormy mood. On the contrary, it is the permission to accept that the stormy mood is a part of you and no one else is responsible for it, nor should be punished by it. It is the grace of understanding that it is *only* a stormy mood and so it, too, shall pass. And you realize that this mood is only a small part of who you are and, relying on that, you may release it more easily. Understanding and loving yourself for all that you are, the wonder of yourself—as well as the parts you may name as bad, less, or not good enough—will gift you with the capacity to accept and love others for being who they are, and all that entails.

> *Seeing and embracing your true nature, accepting the flaws, strengths, dreams, and fears that make up who you are, allows you the generosity to understand others.*

Seeing and embracing your true nature, accepting the flaws, strengths, dreams, and fears that make up who you are, allows you the generosity to understand others.

Every child has the potential to be a powerful force of good in the world. If you, as the adult, empower your child to develop into that potential, you have given your child, yourself, and the world you live in a gift beyond measure—a positive person believing in and doing good for themselves and others. In order to nurture this natural unfoldment of personal worth in children it is essential that you, as a parent and educator, first examine your own sense of self-worth.

As a parent I can ask myself:

- Do I, myself, have positive self-esteem?
- Do I accept, love, and embrace myself just as I am?
- Can I look at myself, my weaknesses and strengths, and love the whole that they create?
- Do I recognize my accomplishments and failures equally?
- Will I work at adopting this approach, although it may be unfamiliar to me?

What you as a parent can do, for your own betterment and for the betterment of the children, is to practice building healthy self-esteem for yourself first. Only when you begin on this path yourself can you accept and express authentic acknowledgment for others. You teach self-esteem, then, first by example.

Traits of Children with High Self-Esteem	Traits of Children with Low Self-Esteem
• Cooperative, team players • See self as source of successes • Creative problem solvers • Open for input • Set own standards • Have many friends • Responsible • Know strengths and weaknesses • Have leadership skills • Proud of accomplishments • Generally have a positive attitude	• Usually reluctant to be involved • Fault others for their failures • Concentrate on fears and problems • Avoid challenging situations • Constantly compare self to others • Withdrawn and often very shy • Blame others and feel guilty • Are defensive • Rarely offer information • Concentrate on failures • Generally have a negative attitude

Core Success Tools for You

Self-Esteem

Children with a strong sense of self-esteem not only feel good about themselves, they know they belong, know they are unique, and they have a sense of their own power.

Some questions you can ask your children to open a discussion about Raising Self-Esteem are:

- Who am I?
- Do I like myself? Why or why not?
- Do I believe that I am good just as I am? Why or why not?
- How well do I treat myself? How do I allow myself to be treated?
- Do I appreciate the uniqueness of others and treat them accordingly?

The three distinct areas that we can focus on at home and as parents to help raise and strengthen our children's self-esteem are their sense of connectedness, their uniqueness, and their sense of power. Naturally, these all blend together in our inner world, but we can work directly with each area to promote self-esteem and personal empowerment. Let's look at each in turn.

Connectedness

Children who have a feeling of connectedness know they are a part of the group whether it is the family, class at school, club, or community. They know that they belong and can contribute something of value. They also believe this about others in the group, thereby contributing to the group's cohesiveness. They include others in games or projects, or offer their own help when others have begun something. The current fad of exclusion is a perfect example of a generation not having a sense of connectedness. They believe that they are only acceptable when they belong to a certain clique, and at the same time exclude or mistreat certain others, who are not deemed good enough for that same clique.

Although bonding by exclusion is a form of group building that can bond the individuals in the group to one another, is not based on a sense of feeling good, but rather upon a false sense of belonging and of fear that, at some point, they too will not belong. In such a situation, there is an unspoken, vague catalog of requirements of the group, which can be changed or annulled at any time. Those persons actively excluded from the group are bullied, usually verbally, either directly or behind their back, and are left with a very poor sense of worth and connectedness. By enhancing the sense of belonging of all children, and especially their awareness that you are, indeed, ALL connected in one way or another, such destructive group activities will vastly decrease.

There was an interesting experiment done by a group of college students in southern California in the late 1970s. They planted a person at a lunch table in the cafeteria of a school. This person's job was to notice behavior whenever there was gossiping or exclusion taking place. Then, if the exclusion became a group dynamic instead of only a one- or two-person conversation, the plant's job was to interject something positive about the person being verbally excluded. And, the results were fascinating. In almost all of the cases, there were a number of people in the group who would participate in the gossip and verbal exclusion of the person. However, if the plant, only one single voice, said something positive, the gossip and exclusion stopped. Not only that, in many instances, it actually turned around. Individuals who had remained quiet used the positive statement as a springboard to say something positive about the person that had just been gossiped about. This dynamic would indicate that exclusion as well as inclusion are group behaviors that can be influenced or even directed. So, why not use it to your advantage and teach your kids to speak a good word whenever possible!

Core Success Tools for You

Connectedness

Some ways that you can help your child feel more accepted and connected are to:

- Be sincerely interested, present, and authentic when interacting and communicating with your child; turn off the TV, put down the phone or paper and be with your child.
- Give acknowledgment to your child when possible.
- Name your child's accomplishments in detail, and express them in relation to his/her own measures, not by another's.
- Express acceptance and affection for your child, verbally, physically, and with your actions.
- Assign tasks that highlight the strengths and strengthen the weaknesses of your child.
- Create discussion times in the family when feelings are shared, such as mealtimes or on car rides. Encourage your child to address difficulties in the family or at school, and to help each other solve problems (in Chapter 3, Living to Thrive, see activity Family Meetings).
- Include your child who doesn't feel connected into family activities (especially if withdrawn) or give child tasks to include him/her in a family project.

Uniqueness

Children who feel their worth as a person know that they, like every other person, are unique and special. They do not compare themselves to others, but rather measure their successes, strengths, and weaknesses according to their own internal guidelines. They accept themselves as whole, unique individuals. They are able, then, to offer this type of acceptance to others as well.

Whether you have one or seven children (or more!), each one of them is unique. Having that sense of individuality and specialness allows especially developing children to feel they have something special to bring to their family, their group of friends, and their community. The special way a person thinks, looks, and laughs; the talents he/she has; the sense of humor; and way of seeing and being in the world are what makes each person unique. Magnifying those special traits regularly allows children to feel a sense of celebration for their uniqueness. That is a very powerful contribution to a child's growing sense of self-esteem.

Core Success Tools for You

Uniqueness

Some ways that an adult can facilitate a child's feeling of value and uniqueness are to:

- Accentuate your child's strengths by speaking them when you see them; play down weaknesses by suggesting steps for improvement and expressing your faith in their ability to transform them;
- Look for and support areas of special interest or ability;
- Emphasize talents;
- Acknowledge your child in front of others;
- Discuss the importance of seeing mistakes as learning opportunities and the necessity of missing the mark while practicing a skill—model seeing your own mistakes as learning opportunities!
- Designate a special and prominent area in the home where your child can display their work successes and ideas;
- Avoid correcting your child in front of others, waiting instead until the situation has passed or seeking out a one-on-one talk;
- Do exercises and have discussions to help your child (1) define and appreciate herself, and (2) describe and aspire to your child's desires and dreams.

Personal Power

All of us have incredible power within. That life force has created who we are. Tapping into that power, or rediscovering it, contributes to your self-image and sense of self-worth. For a child to know that he has strength and clarity, the power to decide, to move forward, to choose directions, to affect a change, and to make a difference in the world helps him to feel he is in charge of his own life. He is not a victim of circumstances but rather the key player in the game of his own life. Feeling that sense of power allows a child, not to mention adults, to take action and make decisions from a place of ease and self-knowledge rather than from doubt or insecurity.

People who sit in their own sense of power have no need to push themselves on others or to use force to go after what they desire. As contradictory as it sounds, anger and bullying can be seen as an expression by people who feel out of control and are seeking a sense of power for themselves. Encouraging kids to develop their sense of power gives them a calm and reliable sense of stability within as they navigate their world, thus eliminating the need to control anyone or anything other than themselves.

"Encouraging a child means that one or more of the following critical life messages are coming through, either by word or by action: I believe in you, I trust you, I know you can handle this, You are listened to, You are cared for, You are very important to me."

BARBARA COLOROSO

Core Success Tools for You

Personal Power

Here are some ways you can facilitate your child's experience of his/her own sense of power.

- Plan activities that emphasize the power of each person, such as having a child with a good sense of direction lead the way on a hike, or a child who is a clear decision-maker guide others in the family to learn how to make their own decisions;
- Help your child define goals, and then devise a game plan for achieving them;
- Acknowledge and celebrate personal successes at school, in sports and hobbies, and at home;
- Encourage your child to make her own decisions. Discuss the process of decision making in detail. Assist unsure children by limiting the choices when decisions are made (this is necessary with younger children in any case);
- Define time and its freedoms and restrictions with your child. Help him learn to work with and manage it;
- Design with your child a tracking system she can use for improvement and successes;
- Accent the process of improving rather than the goal achieved.

Self-Image

How you see yourself plays a large role in how you feel about, and esteem, yourself. Many of us do not allow ourselves to feel really great about ourselves. You may say you long to feel good, that you want to finally stop beating yourself up for this or that perceived weakness or flaw. But do you ever allow yourself to finally arrive at feeling great about yourself? Usually not and as you know all too well, you can't teach something that you, yourself, don't know how to do. So, in order to help your children see themselves in a positive light, to feel really great about who they are, you have to—you guessed it—do so for yourself! And, here's your chance to start.

Core Success Tools for You

Self-Image

Here's a simple exercise you can do to improve your sense of power and self-esteem. After you've completed it, you can walk your child through the steps as well.

What's Best about ME . . .

1. Reserve a quiet evening for yourself. Literally, put "quiet evening" in your calendar as you do your doctor's appointment or tire change date. Now, turn your attention kindly toward yourself. Sit down with a pen and paper and create a list of the best things about yourself—things you like about yourself and things you can do well. Allow yourself to be honest, acknowledging all the things you have going for you. You're allowed to speak well of yourself!

2. Next go look in the mirror. Yes, get up and go look in the mirror. Imagine what others may see in you, or what positive feedback you have heard. Now go back and write down these things as well.

3. Next, on a different piece of paper write a list of things you would like to change about yourself, things you'd like to learn or do differently. Be sure to make assessments instead of judgments. Here is the difference between an assessment-based and a judgment-based desire:
   - Assessment-based: I'd like to improve my note reading and learn to play an entire piece of music on the piano.
   - Judgment-based: I stink at reading music and want to, at the very least, be able to play one single piece of music on the piano.

4. After you have your list of attributes you admire about yourself and of things you'd like to change, post them both in a prominent place in your home. Read them frequently and give yourself acknowledgment for what you have already accomplished and become. Then acknowledge yourself for striving to be the best person you can be. Take your hat off to yourself for having goals and being willing to work toward them.

Treating yourself with this kind of respect and recognition will take you farther down the road of success in feeling great and having positive self-esteem than would judging yourself and tearing yourself down. And, isn't it your goal to build yourself up and to feel good? Isn't that what you want for your kids as well? This is a plan on how to practice and achieve just that.

The Mistake Misnomer

The fear of making mistakes or, put differently, the intense need to always know the answer or to do it right, hinders your ability to learn. Truly believing you have to have the answer, or that it has to be done perfectly the first time, stops you from figuring it out. Children are not exempt from this strong desire to "do it right." Yet this behavior, which is learned from the people (ahem!) and events in their lives, can be unlearned. Trusting yourself to do the best you can and to believe that, with practice, you can master your task is key to the learning process and especially to the joy involved in that process. This can only take place, however, when we adults first eradicate our own fear of making mistakes, doing it wrong, embarrassing ourselves, or not feeling we are good enough.

Let's take the case of learning to write the alphabet. The first time you printed the letter "t" it certainly did not resemble the "t" you can now pen. The hook at the bottom was either nonexistent or too big, giving the impression of an umbrella, or the cross bar was floating in air, or sitting on the hook. These first attempts helped us realize that it just didn't look right and needed to be done differently. Perhaps you needed to shift your paper, adjust the pencil lower in your hand, or relax your shoulder. Every "t" was not a mistake. On the contrary, each was another opportunity to finely tune that letter, until the day that most of your "t's" looked, well, like "t's"!

So, indeed, mistakes are misunderstood; they are not something that we should fear, shun, or hide. They are an essential component of the learning process. The only way *to* learn is by: diving in, doing your best, seeing how far off you are of the goal, learning from each attempt, coming to realize how you can do it better, and then practicing, practicing, practicing. Eventually, you master your task.

Formulating Feelings

Humans are blessed with a complex nature of a logical mind and big emotions. With varied possibilities of expressing your emotions (from the Latin *to move*), formulating feelings can take many forms. Before you are able to express what you are feeling, you must first be able to sense your feelings, to define them, before you can move to the next step of expressing them in a manner beneficial to you. Feelings are always moving and motivating you, whether you are aware of them or not. Taking the time to first become clear about their presence and then train how to communicate them well will greatly

The fear of making mistakes or, put differently, the intense need to always know the answer or to do it right, hinders your ability to learn.

assist you in dealing with people and events in your life. Doing so will also help you develop and maintain healthy and nurturing relationships with others.

There is a tendency to assume that certain feelings such as happiness, contentment, and relaxation are "good," and feelings such as anger, resentment, and agitation are "bad." Feelings are categorized this way firstly because of what you experience when you have them, but also you judge feelings this way because of what you have learned, because of your beliefs and your social norms. Yet, judging them that way cuts you off from their validity and, hence, from dealing with them effectively. By judging what you feel, you divorce yourself from the process of intimately knowing what you feel, and from expressing it in a healthy and appropriate manner.

And, judging feelings doesn't make them go away. You actually confuse a situation by judging what you are feeling. No matter how they could be categorized, it is by being aware of all of your feelings that you can much better define them. When you have that awareness, you are then able to take responsibility and ownership of your feelings. All feelings along the spectrum of emotion are part of your humanness. They are important in the scheme of life. It is useful to embrace them so that you can then deal with them in a healthy manner.

Also, getting to know the triggers and causes of your feelings is very helpful in raising your awareness. This practice helps you get to know, accept, and love yourself. When you learn how to identify and then express your emotions, you master the art of well-being and good relations.

Identifying in which situations you experience which feelings is hugely helpful. You are then better able to understand your child and to help them understand and navigate their own feelings. You can practice tools to verbally and physically express feelings in a way that honors you and those you are interacting with. Respect for your own inner world, for your feelings, and also for the feelings of others is a sign of emotional maturity.

Using "I Messages" as opposed to "You Messages" is essential in the expression phase of knowing your feelings. Briefly, since this will be covered in Chapter 6, *Resolving Conflict*, a "You Message" is what most often leads to conflict. When one speaks about what the other person did, or thinks, usually formulated with accusations and assumptions it is called a "You Message." An "I Message" speaks clearly from one's own perspective and refrains from accusations and assumptions. It is respectful and goes a long way to prevent conflict and maintain respectful communication. Practicing that kind of communication is almost miraculous in the changes it creates.

The Art of Acknowledgment

Kids hear everything you say, but they hear criticism a lot louder.
HARRY SHEEHY

Acknowledgment can be defined as the act of accepting, or recognizing, a fact—the importance or quality of something or someone. It is expressing or displaying gratitude for, or appreciation of, that person or thing. It is based on acceptance of the person and the knowledge that the person is doing her absolute best in all situations, given what she has learned, currently believes, and is presently capable of. Acknowledge the good and eliminate blame from the equation.

You need to differentiate between using acknowledgment to express that you accept and value someone as a person, and using praise as a ploy to influence someone. If children are confident in who they are, compared only with their own performance or standards, then you are giving them a gift of believing in themselves and encouraging them to strive toward improvement because it feels good to them. You are acknowledging them. If they feel good about themselves and their own accomplishments, there is no urge to be better than others. It is enough to be good according to their own standards. Acknowledging children and encouraging them to keep on their track is also an effective process to uphold their natural love of learning.

If, on the other hand, you use your own opinion as a standard, and/or compare their accomplishments to others, and pack it in "nice" words, they develop an attitude of competition or sense of not being "good enough." Comparison often creates the feeling of internal pressure to meet external demands. Unhealthy and unstructured competition breeds contempt among siblings, students, and friends whereas constructive acknowledgment keeps the focus and personal satisfaction on doing one's own job well and accomplishing that which one sets forth to do. Other people's opinions then carry less weight and there is no striving only in order to do better than the other guy. Acknowledgment does not mean you ignore areas of improvement or point out what went wrong. It does mean, though, that in doing so you focus on what went right while encouraging improvement in other aspects.

By acknowledging you need to first observe, in detail, how a person behaves or what he has done. Then you share your observations with him in words or actions. You can, therefore, encourage and remind others when they are down and have lost sight of their beauty. Hearing affirming words regularly can support one's personal sense of well-being. Acknowledgment, when used as a tool for better relations and building self-esteem, lets people feel confirmed, especially after they have invested time and energy into something. Being acknowledged gives you a mirror in which you can see your own accomplishments reflected back to you. This keeps you focused on doing your best according to your own standards and striving toward self-set goals. When you are acknowledged this way, you can then sit back and observe what you have done with a sense of satisfaction: "Yes, I have worked hard and my efforts have paid off," or, "Well, it isn't perfect, but I have improved a lot since last time." Practicing this form of acknowledgment will go a long way toward raising your child's self-esteem.

Core Success Tools for You

The Art of Self-Acceptance

Simple statements that observe in detail a person's efforts, mirror what you see about them, or recognize their improvement are valuable tools to build solid self-acceptance.
For example:

- You have worked all morning without giving up. That is determination.
- You completed that art project exactly according to the directions your teacher gave you. Good follow-through.
- What an imaginative idea. No doubt you will be able to implement it.
- I see that you have given your best on this homework.
- Even though it didn't go as well as you wished, you're working at it diligently and that shows your desire to succeed. I believe in you.

The environment will never cease giving you information and feedback. That is how you learn about the world, how people think, and how you are perceived. It is, therefore, highly useful when you build and maintain strong self-esteem to filter out any judgment from "out there" that you are not OK. Judgments that you are not OK are purely statements from the speaker's viewpoint and are not an accurate assessment of who you are. The fact is that your value as a person is never tarnished by your actions, even when others, or even yourself, view them as "wrong" or undesirable. Your acknowledgment is one way of offering your child a positive environment to counter balance what the world at large offers up—a connected parent can offset negative feedback.

External Orientation vs. Internal Orientation

When you use self-awareness, instead of comparison, and have a strong sense of self-acceptance, built with the aid of acknowledgment, you are equipped with an internal navigation system that shows you how to maneuver through the events of your day. Since you are the one living your life, it is important that this map is one that you have self-designed, know intimately, can navigate, or can change at will. Learning to trust your own assessment and taking self-determined action is a process in which you can practically support your children. Dynamic trust in yourself is trust that is constantly challenged, questioned, confirmed, and relied upon on a daily basis. Being acknowledged buoys the trust in your own abilities to take care of yourself, and to do your personal best, especially in the home environment.

The Words You Use

Change your words and you change your world,
for your words create your world.

Language is the most effective tool humans possess to communicate needs, feelings, ideas, and thoughts. From birth onward you experience language as a form of interaction. It is our only direct means—other than touch—to convey our inner world with others. In learning any language the first phase that takes place is passive understanding, then comes a limited application of the broader passive knowledge, and then active mastery of the language, using it as a tool for precise communication.

How does language create your view of the world?

There is not a moment during your waking hours when a constant dialogue is not taking place inside your head. Stop reading this sentence now and listen for a moment to what your inner conversation is about. What is the subject matter and what are your opinions? Usually this dialogue goes unnoticed. Occasionally you click into it so as to share what you are just thinking, or to take action on a current thought. However, although the vast majority of the dialogue rambles on unnoticed, you are still constantly acting from its content. This constant dialogue, and the language used in it, determines how you see yourself, see others, and designs your very concept of the world. The language you use becomes the architect of your reality and the filter of your experiences.

How do others hear you?

As the speaker in conversation with others you first select the thoughts you want to share and then formulate them as you wish. Then you choose the words to impart those ideas to whom you are speaking. Depending on the language you choose, the conversation will take on different taints, pictures, and directions. In addition to your body language with its unspoken intention, what you are verbally expressing is being filtered by the receiving lens of the person listening to you. And their filter is formed according to their personal history, definition of certain words, current perspective and emotional state, and how they decipher your nonverbal communication. These factors determine how your words land this way, or that way, in the listener's perception. Seen in this light it is amazing two people can communicate at all! In any case, communication is truly a challenge and an art of understanding one another.

How different self-talk affects you

A failed test:

You failed the last test you took in math. There are a myriad of ways that you could choose to look at this situation and consequently dialogue with yourself about it. One possibility is:

1. "Man, I am dumb! I knew a lot of those answers and I stupidly rushed through and got so many wrong. I don't even need to try again because I'll do the same thing again. Man, I'm a loser."

Another possibility is:

2. "What a drag. I knew a lot of those answers! If I'd taken the time I could've answered almost every one correctly. I *know* I can do better. The next time I'm going to concentrate on going more slowly and really focus. I know whenever I really work at something I can always improve. Next time I'll ace it."

Clearly, depending on which of these inner dialogues you choose to engage in, your attitude following the test results will certainly be different. And the outcome of the next test will also be different. It's only a matter of willingness to speak highly of yourself and to practice words that build your self-worth.

I wasn't invited to the party:

Five friends from your tennis club were invited to a friend's birthday party, and you were not. One possibility to dialogue with yourself about this is:

1. "I thought I was one of his friends, too. He really doesn't like me; if he did, he would have invited me as well. Well, I'll show him. I'll just not be his friend either. He can play the next tournament alone. Anyway, who needs his birthday party?"

Another possibility is:

2. "Boy, I'd really like to go to his birthday party. I wonder why he invited the others and not me. I thought we were friends. Kind of makes me feel left out and not liked. If I get a chance, I'm going to ask him about it. I'd like to at least know his reasons why. And if I'm really not invited, we can still be friends. Heck, we're on the same team. But it's his party and he can invite whom he wants to."

Core Success Tools for You

The Words You Use

Using words that take away your power bring you down and confirm a belief about yourself that then continues to disempower you, hence creating a downward spiral.

There's a simple tool called The Law of Displacement that requires only alertness to the thoughts you think. It merely entails replacing one thought that generates bad feelings and bombards your mind with thoughts that create good feelings instead. It's helpful to put these thoughts into writing so that the recognition and replacement become easier. Make a list of your self-talk, of that constant chatter of those words that don't do you any good. Then for each of those words or phrases, write down three new ones to counter, and practice, practice, practice.

For example:

- I can't.
- I don't know.
- There's no hope.
- It's all over.
- I don't have a chance.
- I give up.

By re-training yourself to use different words you shift your focus and with it your world and experiences become more powerful and useful to you.

For example:

- I can if I work at it; I can do anything; if I want to, I can.
- I have the answer; I'll figure it out; I just need to look for it.
- There is always a way; I won't give up; tomorrow is a new chance.
- Anything is possible; every ending is a beginning; no means "next."
- I am blessed with opportunities; I've got something special to offer; why not me?
- Now I've got it; I'll never give up; I'm determined.

Positively languaging yourself is trainable and attainable. Tomorrow during quiet times, before getting out of bed, while driving to work, eating your lunch, allow words to float through your mind that are uplifting: happiness, joy, contentment, peace, harmony, excitement, accomplished, tranquility, connectedness. Whatever words are meaningful and uplifting to you, let them filter into your consciousness. Practice that for 30 days and you will see a vast difference in how you feel and see yourself and the world.

The Lure of Listening

Listening, not just hearing but truly listening, to someone is one of the greatest gifts you can give to a person. Being such a crucial factor in all communication and relationships, listening is covered frequently in this book, and more specifically in Chapter 6, *Resolving Conflict*.

Tuning into your own inner dialogue first, and really listening to it, can profoundly benefit not only your listening ability but your quest in building a more positive self-image—doing so you hear what your thoughts convey about your self-concept and your view of the world. Next you can shift your focus to tune into what people around you are saying. Actively listening to what they are expressing, and reflecting back to them in order to confirm accuracy, will give you insight into who they are, and how they see their world. It will also give you the opportunity to connect to them and support them better.

As parents you have a profound responsibility to honor what your children share with you, and with each other. Listening deeply to your children reminds you that they are still sharing from a place of purity. Hearing what they directly, and indirectly, say is a valuable tool in helping them build a connection between you and them, as well as build a stronger sense of self.

This process of actively listening is actually less time consuming than what we as parents usually do: hearing on the fly what is being said, asking them to repeat it once or more, not getting the message, or misunderstanding, then doing the whole thing over again until clarity prevails. This quality of listening will open up worlds for children, and for the listener as well. It is the first step in building trust.

Core Success Tools for You

Listening to and Speaking to Your Children

When listening to your children:

- Get down to their eye level (or up – my son is 6'4"!).
- Look them in the eye.
- Indicate you are interested.
- Do not interrupt or rush them.
- Listen to what they say without judgment, admonition, or advice.
- Ask for clarification if needed.
- Reflect back what you have heard.

Seeking to understand and then communicating what you understand is very effective. In reflecting back to the speaker what you've heard, you affirm whether your understanding is correct. It also lets the other person know you are listening.

When speaking to your children, you can say:

- If I understand you correctly, you feel that....
- I think I understand. Is it that you … ?
- It looks like you are sure that ....
- It is difficult when that happens. How can I assist you?
- Oh, you mean that; you hoped that; they would.
- That is important for you, I know. Thank you for telling me about it.
- It sounds to me like you are sad about …
- You look really happy. Did you say that …?
- I think that you would like…. Is that correct, or do you want something else?
- I'm not sure I understand. Could you repeat that please?
- It is important to me to really listen to you and I am busy now. Could you share it with me in 10 minutes?
- So, you are angry that happened. Is that right?

I'd like to share this poem with you that really says it all…

Please Just Listen to Me

When I ask you to listen to me, and you start giving advice,

You have not done what I asked.

When I ask you to listen to me, and you begin
to tell me why I shouldn't feel that way,

You are trampling on my feelings.

When I ask you to listen to me, and you feel you
have to do something to solve my problem,

You have failed me, strange as that may seem.

Listen! All I asked, was that you listen,

Not talk or do—just hear me.

And I can do for myself; I'm not helpless. Maybe
discouraged and faltering, but not helpless.

When you do something for me that I can and need to
do for myself, you contribute to my fear and weakness.

But, when you accept as a simple fact that I do
feel what I feel, no matter how irrational,

Then I can quit trying to convince you

And can get about the business of understanding
what's behind this irrational feeling.

And when that's clear, the answers are
obvious and I don't need advice.

Irrational feelings make sense when we
understand what's behind them.

Perhaps that's why prayer works, for some
people. Because God is mute, and

He doesn't give advice or try to fix things.

He just listens and lets you work it out for yourself.

So, please listen and just hear me.

And, if you want to talk, wait a minute for
your turn; and I'll listen to you.

Ray Houghton, MD, "Teen Times," Nov/Dec 1979

As parents, caretakers, and teachers, it is vital that you be authentic and purposeful in your interactions with your children. Every interaction you have with your child is literally another practice session in the formation of his self-image and self-worth. You can create the circumstances and environment that will help your children form a strong, positive, and healthy sense of self. You do so by the language you use and the way you impart information, acknowledgment, and critique. What is essential is a deep acceptance of the person you are as you speak to your child. A keen awareness of what you say and, especially, how you say it is crucial.

Core Success Tools for You

Strengthening Self-Esteem

You can help build your child's self-esteem in the following ways:

- Use your child's name only in a kind voice. If you're angry, don't use her name.
- Give a lot of hugs.
- Have one-to-one conversations with your child every day.
- Provide multiple ways for your child to feel successful and needed at home.
- Display your child's work and ideas around the house.
- Give your child a responsibility at home.
- Speak positively about your child to others and in his presence.
- Take time to point out the positive aspects of your child's efforts.
- Never criticize your child's question.
- Take time to help struggling kids understand.
- Help your child turn failure into a positive learning experience.
- Encourage your child to take risks.
- Provide opportunities for your child to make her own decisions about certain aspects of your home life, such as, how to decorate the dining table, the destination of the next family outing, etc.
- Provide opportunities for siblings to work with each other.
- Be curious. Don't make assumptions about a child's behavior. Ask sincere questions.
- Allow your child to experience the consequences of his behavior – don't be overly protective.
- Allow your child to explore options in different situations.
- Celebrate your child's achievements, no matter how small!
- Before bedtime take time to acknowledge the things you saw and heard your child doing well that day.

Conclusion

Being personally involved in the process of building self-esteem, and then helping your children do so for themselves, will simultaneously facilitate them to contribute to positive self-esteem in others. And in order to accept others for who they are, you must first accept yourself for who you are. It is a self-perpetuating process.

Feeling good about oneself not only assures a satisfying and enjoyable life, but strong self-esteem creates positive relationships with others. Valuing yourself offers you the insight and ability to value others. High self-esteem is the foundation for peaceful inter-actions among people and for personal core success.

CORE Success Factors of Raising Self-Esteem

CLARITY	OWNERSHIP	RESOLUTION	EXCELLENCE
Define self-concept Strengthen self-esteem Identify traits of self-esteem Build positive self-image	Choose posi-tive attitude Know and express feelings Accept yourself Be wise with words you use	Disempower mistakes Use acknowledgment Listen	Build connectedness Build uniqueness Build power Practice tools to raise self-esteem

Keys to CORE Success

♂ Self-esteem is the foundation of emotional well-being.

♂ Self-esteem enables people to build healthy and peaceful relationships.

♂ As adults, you must re-train your own interaction habits.

♂ What I think then becomes true in my perception.

♂ There is a stark difference between boasting and self-recognition.

♂ Competition with others is a trap. Compare only with one's own measurement of success.

♂ Mistakes are mandatory.

♂ Accept others for who they are, not what they do.

♂ Use the tools.

Challenges and FAQs

✓ *I struggle with my own self-esteem, how can I help my child build their own?* Not many adults have a healthy sense of self-esteem, so you are not alone. Especially if you feel chal-lenged in this area, practice some of these tools with yourself first. Find ways to feel your own uniqueness, connectedness, and power. Do the suggested *CORE Success Tools for You* exercises in this chapter on a weekly basis until your lists grow longer and until being appreciative of yourself becomes a sincerely comfortable thing for you to do.

✓ I also urge you to become aware of how you speak to yourself. Start a list of the phrases you use when addressing yourself and your actions, such as, *How dumb can you be? Man, I'm a loser. I never get it right*, etc. When your patterns become apparent, apply the suggestions in the *CORE Success Tools for You* exercise also in this chapter in your self-talk. Remember the SOADA steps of self-awareness? See, own, accept, decide, and act. Do that with these tools to build self-esteem for yourself and you can literally be the change you wish to see in your family!

✓ *My teenage daughter thinks all this positive reinforcement is uncool and fake.* If you spend some time listening to how these young people speak to one another, you will understand the source of their skepticism. Nonetheless, persevere. However, be very aware of your authenticity. If you don't think they did a good job cleaning up their room, then acknowledge them for making an effort. If you see their attention to homework is slacking off, speak to them of the potential you see in them and that you know they can pull of better grades if they wanted to. A trainer I once had taught me to believe in, speak to, and act according to the highest potential I see in my children and they will align themselves with that picture of themselves. The teen years can be challenging for many reasons, but the need to feel good about one's self and the desire to have our parents believe in us does not wane during that time. If anything, it increases.

✓ *How can I help my child to believe in himself when he's getting the daily message from "out there" that he is only okay, if he does xyz?* Being the singular, kind yet honest measure of one's own self-worth is the very heart of self-esteem. There will always be input from outside of ourselves—some great, some not. The art is to listen to what is said and take from it the critique that is useful—according to one's own value system—and leave the rest behind, knowing it is a statement only about the speaker's perspective and not about one's own value.

For years I had been told I was a tyrant. Those comments continued to cripple my self-esteem. During my process of transformation, I decided to look at that consistent feedback for any truth as seen through the filter of my own value system. What a gift that was. I came to see that I had learned to use anger to feel my power, and also to motivate myself. Through that self-reflection I also discovered that was not the way I wanted to feel powerful or move myself forward. So, being a student of myself, I worked at it and changed that pattern until my behavior aligned with my values of respect and kindness, toward others and myself. Making that change helped me eliminate my need to use anger at all and drastically increased my self-esteem.

ANCHOR WITH ACTIVITIES

....
I Can

What's the point?

To help children develop an awareness and appreciation of all the things they *can* do.

What do I need?

Chart paper, markers/pencils/colored pencils, tin cans (emptied with one end removed and labels off), white paper cut to fit around the tin can

What do I do?

Put the words I CAN at the top of the chart paper. List the things that you can do. Ask children to tell you some things they can do, or have them list them in their CORE Success Notebook.

Examples could be:

- I can sing
- I can swim
- I can jog 1 mile
- I can ride a skateboard
- I can cook
- I can speak Italian

Have children write and or draw things that they can do on the white paper provided. Have them work horizontally on the paper (so it will fit around the can)—just the word or phrase is sufficient, there is no need for the word I CAN to be put on the can. Have children color and decorate their cans, which can be used around the house, for example, to put pencils in or as a flower vase.

Note: Put the cans on display next to a tent card with the title in large letters "THINGS I CAN DO." Share the cans with friends.

How do I continue the conversation?

- How did you feel doing this activity?
- Did you learn more about yourself?
- Do you appreciate what you can do now?

Take it a step further

Self-esteem banners: Cut a large piece of paper to resemble a flag banner or vertical banner; draw three circles on it. The child's name will go on the side of the flag banner or on the top of the vertical banner. In the first circle children put "Things I can do" (then make a list under the heading), second circle is "Things I want to learn to do" (then make list under this heading), and third circle is for a photo or drawing of themselves. The banner can be decorated and colored once children have completed the circles.

Ex-haling Experiences

What's the point?

To develop an awareness and understanding that how we treat others is crucial in helping to build or destroy their self-esteem. That it is important to be empathetic toward others.

What do I need?

Ex-haling Experiences Story (see Appendix), chart paper, markers, one balloon for each person, story (see below), CORE Success Notebook, pencils

What do I do?

Pass out a balloon to each person. Ask each person to blow up the balloon but do not tie a knot in the end. They are to hold it well in their fingers with it blown up but the end untied. Then, do the following activity:

Speaker says: "Our self-esteem is how we feel about ourselves. How good we feel about ourselves is often affected by how others treat us. If somebody is nasty to us, teases us, puts us down, rejects us, hits us, etc., then some of our self-esteem is destroyed. I am going to tell you a story to illustrate how this happens in everyday life."

Proceed to tell the children about a boy, or a girl, who is about the same age as your children are. An outline is provided below. Pick a name that no one is familiar with. As you tell the story, be as emotional and dramatic as you can. You will have to fill it in with your own imagination. As you describe each event that negatively affects the "made up" child's self-esteem, ask each person to let some air out of the balloon. A possible outline for the story follows. Feel free to adapt, add to, and change in any way you want. (You can have the children help create the story as you go along.) Here we have chosen a girl.

Read the story Ex-haling Experiences to the family. You can think of other examples to help you, if you want to add to the storyline.

- Being picked last to play ball at recess.
- Being picked on by bullies on the way home from school.
- Missing a lot of shots at basketball practice and being laughed at.
- Having a sibling make fun of a trait.

As the story ends, showing the child going to bed with very deflated self-esteem, there should be little or no more air in the balloons. When you finish, ask the following questions, which can be written on chart paper and children can answer in their CORE Success Notebooks or in a family discussion:

- How does *your* balloon get deflated?
- What things affect you the most?

- What do you do that deflates the self-esteem of others—at home, in school, playing sports?
- How do you feel when your self-esteem is deflated? When you deflate someone else's?
- What can we do to help people enlarge their balloons (build their self-esteem) rather than make it smaller?

Take it a step further

Share and discuss answers to these questions. Have everyone think about one thing that they will do each day to help build someone's self-esteem. For a certain time period, a week or 14 days, ask each family member each day to share what they did and the effect it had on the person.

CHAPTER 5

Discipline with Dignity

Children nowadays love luxury, have bad manners,
have contempt for authority, have disrespect for elders,
contradict their parents, talk in front of company,
gobble up their food, and tyrannize their teachers.
SOCRATES, 470 B.C.

In order for any group of people to live and work well together—
in a manner that feels good to all; is respectful; allows for work to
get done, fun to be had, and healthy relationships to develop—
a common theme of group dynamic, life and work philosophy,
self-discipline, and group discipline are mandatory. From the
Aboriginal tribes to the Amish of Pennsylvania, every culture that
works well together has a code of conduct and clear rules that are
known and adhered to by all. If there are infractions, they are dealt
with in a useful way for the entire community to continue functioning in a healthy manner. That is the goal of *Discipline with
Dignity*: to maintain a safe, healthy, cooperative, and happy home.

The Core Point ... and Your Gain

Discipline —the holy grail of raising children, or so it is assumed. All modules of CORE Success' work together so that discipline is no longer the heavy weight we've come to know it as. Instead, discipline can be seen as the strong foundation upon which you build your family, like the foundation for a house. Discipline, then, holds the family structure firmly, yet with love and respect, and allows for life to unfold and thrive within the home.

The factors of discipline that are addressed in *Discipline with Dignity* are:

Defining cooperative discipline, differentiating between consequences and punishment, making rules, creating connected relationships, engaged communication, the home environment, understanding and turning around misbehavior, and defining rights, responsibilities, and the role of goals. As you can see, it's a lot, so let's get started.

Discipline Then and Now

When one reads this chapter's opening quote, it can be rather shocking to realize that it was written so long ago. Not much has changed in this one regard! So the types of behavior that children have, and that are of such concern to us, have been the same for a very long time. However, nowadays you see children as being more disruptive in school, more disrespectful and defiant at home, and more aggressive and violent in general, overall demonstrating less self-control. That *has* changed. And, what has happened to discipline?

A number of critical social factors today have a profound influence; for example, unbridled and uncensored media and its omnipresence; reduced or inadequate adult supervision; lack of spiritual and ethical role models and/or training; decentralized family structures; inconsistent values in society; consumerism; unemployment; and poverty. In addition, our children are bombarded with toxic influences from various sources: television, video games, music, movies, advertising, and Internet websites.

They are all sending messages of disrespect, almost no boundaries, placing the importance of self over others, contempt for authority, materialism, aggression, and violence. All this has desensitized, and demoralized, many of our children. Therefore, it is much more difficult to teach our children to want to behave respectfully and responsibly, to have strong ethics and values, to be empathetic, to treat others with kindness and understanding and show respect for their rights, to stand up against any injustice, and to become strong active citizens and individuals of solid character.

So, the big job of countering all of that lands in our lap at home. To create positive change and to equip our kids with tools that will help them navigate all of these powerful influences, we have to look at the methods that we're using to provide guidance and discipline for our children. Many of the strategies that we presently use are not providing the results we want. It would also be very useful to become acutely aware of the power that you have as parents. It is your mood and approach that creates the environment at home. You are the decisive element. You can humiliate, embarrass, and hurt your kids and make their lives miserable, or you can nurture, heal, motivate, empower, and inspire your children thus making their life at home a joyous one.

It is your mood and approach that creates the environment at home. You are the decisive element. You can humiliate, embarrass, and hurt your kids and make their lives miserable, or you can nurture, heal, motivate, empower, and inspire your children and make their life at home a joyous one.

It is your mood and approach that creates the environment at home. You are the decisive element. You can humiliate, embarrass, and hurt your kids and make their lives miserable, or you can nurture, heal, motivate, empower, and inspire your children and make their life at home a joyous one.

Core Success Tools for You

Discipline Expectations

To better refine your method of discipline and in order to make the most use of this material, it is important to be aware of your own personal philosophy/policy of behavior and discipline. Take a few minutes and write down your expectations and viewpoints on discipline and family management. Please do not write what you think you should be doing or what would be better. Write your current discipline philosophy. You cannot get to where you want to go unless you know precisely where you are now. So start there. This will give you an assessment of your thoughts, beliefs, and actions on behavior and discipline. It will also be your guidepost for your movement forward. No judgment required, just clarity!

1. This is my current philosophy/policy on behaviors and discipline in our home:

    a. What behaviors do I expect?
    b. Do my kids know I expect that behavior? If so, how?
    c. What are my rules?
    d. How do I enforce the rules?
    e. How do I discipline when rules are broken?

2. How consistent am I in my disciplining? Use a scale of 1 – 10, with 1 representing never and 10 representing always.
3. How did you learn/create this policy?

If you're honest about it, what you want as manager of your family is that the family and home are comfortable, cooperative, clean, effective, and fun, but for everyone involved. That means that each person needs to pull their load. I liken your job as a parent to that of being the captain of a large sailing vessel. The ship without the captain and crew is a lifeless thing bobbing in the water. The ship cannot do what it is intended to do, namely sail, or get to where it's going unless the captain is clear about the destination, how to get there, and what jobs need to be done to facilitate arriving safely and in good time. And, the ship won't move without the crew, for if the captain were the sole crew member, having to man the sails, steer the ship, and navigate the seas as a sole agent would be an impossible task. And, if every person on the ship would randomly do whatever job they felt like, at whatever time desired, chaos would reign and nothing would work. In a time of crisis, like a severe storm, the ship would sink under such conditions. A disciplined crew is the only way to assure a safe passage, especially through stormy weather.

That means the captain needs the crew, the crew needs the captain, and they all need trained self-discipline for the ship to be in good working order. The ship's members, captain, and crew are of equal value and equal importance, but each has their own job. Every person is essential to the success of the voyage—so it is with your family as well. You are the captain.

Discipline is as mandatory in your home as it is on that ship. It cannot be stressed enough. The ease and leisure that adults, and children alike, desire is only possible if a strong foundation for self-discipline and cooperative behavior has been laid out ahead of time and integrated into family life consistently for all to be aware of and to abide by.

What is Discipline?

Discipline can be defined in a variety of ways, for example: a system of rules, an area of learning or knowledge, a type of training that develops self-control, orderliness and efficiency, or as treatment that punishes or corrects.

No matter the dictionary definitions, everyone has a very individualized interpretation of the word *discipline*. Depending on your age, cultural background, the parenting style used in your childhood homes, your own parenting style, and your professional area of expertise, this word can have vastly different connotations.

In CORE Success for Parents, I am referring to cooperative discipline. I'll explain. Cooperative discipline is the method of creating a clear, strong, and positive framework to develop useful behavior, which is most effective for a child to establish self-discipline and to contribute to a happy, safe, and cooperative home. This is what CORE Success teaches. Here are its key points:

Cooperative Discipline

- Children are actively involved in *rule making* and examining infractions.

- They train to *take responsibility* for all aspects of their behavior.
- They are confirmed for *making cooperative choices* and for *positive social behavior.*
- Logical *consequences* are used when rules are broken.
- *Self-discipline* is developed from within.
- Cooperative and *respectful relationships* are built.
- *Self-esteem* is valued and left intact and strong.

Children must be taught the values and skills they need in order to become respectful, responsible, and productive adults. They also must be taught how to manage their choices wisely. That, then, is the goal of a good discipline policy at home.

Discipline, Punishment, Consequences

It is important to understand that discipline and punishment are not one in the same. Discipline is used to promote the maturity of knowing what is useful, expected, appropriate, and fair. It builds an internal compass. Punishment, on the other hand, is externally imposed and teaches youth ultimately how to dodge the system. Although punishment may teach children how to behave, they also learn that is serves them best to not get caught committing unwanted behavior. Both discipline and punishment are clear in their intention and execution, as follows:

DISCIPLINE	PUNISHMENT
Comes from within	Imposed by an authority figure
Based on logical consequences	Form of retribution or of inflicting suffering—the violator must pay for an offense
Rules are not negotiable; consequences based on circumstances and situations that may differ	Does not acknowledge different circumstances or situations; rules and punishment are rigid
Is educational in nature; as a teaching strategy, opens options for the individual to choose new behaviors—positive and long-term	Is punitive in nature; as a teaching strategy, it reinforces failure and importance of not getting caught—negative and short-term

DISCIPLINE	PUNISHMENT
Friendly, supportive, firm but fair; respectful in nature	Often characterized by anger, force, and use of power
Intended to build inner strength and discernment; usually results in a more responsible behavior; develops capacity of self-evaluation, of positive social behavior	Intended to control behavior; may increase submissiveness or produce compliance; may lead to rebellion

To be Authoritarian

Individuals who believe in being authoritarian implement a punitive form of discipline, as discussed above. *To be authoritarian means to prefer or to enforce strict obedience often taking place at the expense of personal freedom; to show a lack of concern for another person's desires or views; to be dictatorial* (Oxford University Press, 1998). This is very different than having authority, as discussed below under Cooperative Discipline.

How Can You Create Effective Cooperative Discipline?

If you go back to the Latin roots, **to discipline with authority means to give life to learning**. *Discipline with Dignity,* then, is about bringing life to your children by guiding them to develop self-discipline, which comes from within and is not imposed from the outside. You want your children to make decisions while taking into account many factors including the rights and wants of others. You must teach your children what feels right from within, and help them develop the conscience that asks the question "does this feel good according to my values?" This helps them take a position and act because it's in alignment with their ethics and values. Only then can they be called independent—making decisions that are for the good of all. (See activity Rights and Responsibilities.)

To Have Authority

Creating cooperative discipline entails being aware of the authority you have and wielding it with respect. *To have authority means to have the power or right to give orders; to make decisions; to influence others with one's commanding nature or to be recognized for one's knowledge or expertise; to be confident based on an area of personal expertise* (Oxford University Press, 1998). That sounds like the definition of a parent!

The method used to guide children and your family to self-discipline and to a safe, cooperative, and happy home environment, must be one in which the dignity of the child and that of the adult remain intact. This is how personal CORE Success operates. There are different steps involved in that process. Let's begin.

Core Success Tools for You

Creating Cooperative Discipline

First, become clear, write down and make known:

- What are the family's values?
- What atmosphere is desired in the home?
- Are there special factors that need to be considered, such as, elderly family members, special needs, etc.?
- What kind of work and activities does the family want to enjoy?
- What factors will contribute to those results?
- What behavior is desired?
- What behavior is not acceptable given the family's values?
- What are the rules of the house?
- What consequences could be expected if the rules are not followed?
- What are the responsibilities of the individuals in the home (young and older)?
- How can the family deal with conflict optimally?

Resolving conflicts can be made easier by determining:

- What behavior is unacceptable?
- How they have ownership of the problem.
- How to solve the problems they have created.
- What they can do to make amends.
- What they would do differently next time.
- What they have learned from this experience.

See Chapter 6, *Resolving Conflict,* for more tools and ideas.

With CORE Success the following components lay the foundation of cooperative and effective discipline in the home: making rules, connected relationships, communication, a nurturing home climate, and empowering children.

Making Rules

Creating rules together as a family is going to build your foundation for CORE Success and create and maintain a family life and living environment that is joyful, peaceful, and cooperative. Rules give structure as well as offer safety. Think of traffic rules. What would happen if there were no lines on the streets, no traffic lights, and no one had to indicate when they were turning or could drive as fast or as slowly as they liked? What would the chaos be like? Rules offer us a system for working and living together in groups. Even if the rules are not spoken or laid out, they are there. Making them conscious, useful, and in alignment with the values and mission of your family make them a fantastic tool for a happy home.

Criteria for a good rule

- It is clear, specific, and simply stated so that all can understand.
- It states what is permitted as well as what is not allowed.
- It is easy to distinguish whether or not the rule is broken.
- It is respectful and maintains a child's dignity.

One very effective approach with children of all ages is the concept of empowering them so that they feel ownership of their home environment and feel like an integral part of the family unit. There is no better way to create ownership in a home than to allow children to be a part of the development of the family rules, and consequences where applicable. This also vastly raises the probability of the children cooperating with the rules, because they helped create them! Children can also be involved in creating a plan or contract as to what steps should be taken to change or "turn around" undesired behavior. Allowing them to have genuine input not only gives them ownership, but also a sense of rightness and responsibility to the belief system of the family. This is what is

meant by Cooperative Discipline. (See activity Cooperative Rule Making.) Involving children as rule makers may take more time but it is a worthwhile investment because:
Children help define the standards.

- They have more interest in making the rules work.
- They become more involved in monitoring each other's behavior.
- They have more opportunity to become responsible.
- They learn and apply problem-solving skills.

Creating the rules together with your children is empowering for them, gives you the assurance that they know them, and creates the highest chances of them adhering to them consistently, since they helped create them. The activity Cooperative Rule Making at the end of this chapter will guide you through this process. I recommend that you, or together with your partner, become clear about your own nonnegotiables—meaning, rules and conditions that you are not willing to bend in the home. As the rules are being made together, just keep those predefined ideas in mind and thread them into the activity. You may be very surprised at how well versed your children already are at what rules are helpful and not helpful. Let them take the lead on the creation process while you keep your parameters in mind and use them to form the final result.

Consequences

When teaching appropriate behaviors, consequences may have to be used in certain situations to show that you mean what you say. When the family's code of behavior is broken, consequences are given. These rules are usually more serious in nature so the use of consequences will help to teach children to be responsible. For example, lying about one's whereabouts.

You must also differentiate between punishment and consequences. Most parents wrestle with the distinction between these two. They want their kids to learn what's expected of them, they don't want to inflict harm, yet also do not want to be lenient. What to do? Well, the distinction between the two is not complicated.

In addition, understanding this difference hands you one of the most profound tools for discipline and for your child's learning experience.

CONSEQUENCES	PUNISHMENT
Are the results of an action. They are a logical result of, and directly related to, the rule infringed upon with the intent to be instructional—not punitive.	Causes a person pain, loss, or discomfort for some fault or offense. It is punitive and instills fear while reinforcing the importance of not being caught.

(Oxford English Press, 1998)

Not only do rules have to be clear to children and adults, but the nature of the consequences must be as well. It is important that children are aware of the consequences of specific actions beforehand. For example, if not food is allowed in the bedrooms as a rule (as it is in our home), the kids know the consequence is a thorough (and I mean thorough) cleaning by the child if the rule is broken. This has (almost) completely eliminated eating (and bugs!) in the bedrooms. When implementing consequences, the consequences must be practical and reasonable. They should be simply stated in a calm voice while making direct eye contact with the child. Never embarrass the person receiving the consequence and always be consistent.

Example:

- **Rule:** Dinner is served at 6 P.M. All family members are to be home at 6 for dinner.
- **Behavior:** Skye is late for dinner.
- **Punishment:** Skye is sent to bed without dinner.
- **Consequence:** Skye must heat up her dinner (or prepare it on her own), clean up afterward, and be home 15 minutes early tomorrow evening to ensure that she'll be on time for dinner.

All children need to be treated with fairness; however, this does not mean that they need to be treated equally. A former student of mine said that, "Fairness does not mean that everyone gets the same... Fairness means that everyone gets what they need." Rules and limits are never negotiable, consequences can be.

Core Success Tools for You

Varying Consequences

Anna and Ben

Last Thursday Anna's and Ben's mom, Allison, returned home at 7:30 P.M., after a long day of work. Both children were just finishing the dinner their mom had prepared for them earlier. Allison sat down to be with her children and ask about their day. During the discussion it became clear that Ben had not finished his homework in math or French. Anna had also not completed her assignments in English and geography for the next day. The consequences for neglecting homework is not attending the family movie night on Friday evening, thus giving the children time to complete their homework before the weekend off. Allison decided to sit with each of them individually after they prepared themselves for bed to find out what had caused the errant behavior.

Ben had an unannounced extra basketball practice for the game on Saturday. He first arrived home at 6:00 P.M., after practice. He showered and began his homework immediately. He finished his English homework, but math and French were too much for him to get done before dinner.

Anna's girlfriend Sharon came home with her on the bus. They both decided to do their nails and look at the newest clothing catalogues that came in the mail that day. Anna forgot to look at the clock and first realized the time when Ben came home at 6:00 P.M., after practice. Then it was too little time to get all of her homework done.

Take a moment and think about it. Don't continue reading until you decide what consequences Allison should apply in this case. How would you justify your decision?

In these two cases, consequences would not be the same. However, children have the responsibility to let the parents know if there are extenuating circumstances. Perhaps in this case Ben should have called his mom at work as soon as he found out about the extra practice. I often ask my kids to explain why they chose to behave a certain way, or why they did a certain thing. Often we discuss in detail why they have lied or haven't kept their word. When it seems useful, I ask them what they think a fair consequence would be for them. I always ask what their reasons were and what they will do differently next time. (This is an example of cooperative discipline—getting children involved in the process.) If you'd like more case studies, the book *CORE Success Discipline Guide for Parents* includes more, as well as additional information about rules, consequences, rights, and responsibilities.

Connected Relationships

Discipline should come from both the heart and the head.

Connected relationships are the key to discipline. When people feel connected, they have a willingness to get along and to work with each other on a different level than when they don't have a connection. By connection I mean grooming a relationship where both parties experience trust, caring, safety, and honesty—where telling the truth and being allowed to be, and embraced for, who you are is fundamental to every interaction. That is connection. And, the key to building a good quality atmosphere is to develop strong, connected, positive, mutually respectful relationships with each other. If you create a warm supportive home environment in which everyone feels that their needs are met, and they are accepted and can, therefore, be successful, discipline problems will be vastly diminished.

How much trust your children have in you (and later in dependable others) will greatly influence the interactions and the environment at home. Children discover at a very early age who you are, what you stand for, what you expect from them, and what they can expect from you. They must know your commitment, your expectations, and your limits. Above all, they have to know and believe that you will be there for them!

The Emotional Bank Account

In his book, *Seven Habits of Highly Effective People* (Covey, 1989), Stephen Covey uses an *Emotional Bank Account* as a metaphor that describes the amount of trust and the feeling of safeness that has been built up in a relationship. If I make deposits into an *Emotional Bank Account* with you through courtesy, kindness, honesty, and keeping my commitments to you, I build up a reserve.

Your trust toward me becomes higher and communication between us becomes easy and effective. But if I have a habit of showing discourtesy, disrespect, overreacting, ignoring you, betraying your trust, eventually my *Emotional Bank Account* with you becomes overdrawn. The trust level gets low and I have to be very careful of everything I say.

Communication

Speaking

It is always important when communicating to say what you mean, and mean what you say. Be clear and concise, and then stick to it. Your *choice of words* has an overwhelming effect on the process of communication. To build strong relationships, which lead to cooperative discipline, your communication skills are key.

Core Success Tools for You

Bad/Good Communication Choices

Here are some statements that are poor choices of communication:

- Blaming/accusing: "Look at what you've done. How many times do I have to tell you ..."
- Martyrdom: "When I was your age ..."
- Criticizing: "You always sulk when you're upset."
- Name-calling: "You are such a procrastinator."
- Threatening: "If you don't, I will ..."

Here are some examples of good communication:

- Encouraging: "Can you tell me more? Let's work through it together."
- Clarifying: "When did this happen? Who was involved?"
- Affirming: "You seem very upset. I can understand how you feel."
- Validating: "I appreciate your willingness to resolve this matter."

It has been said that parents often talk too much to their children, and at their children, rather than with their children. It is not only what you say, but also how you say it.

I have become aware of a personal paradox; I often use tactics similar to those that I try to eradicate in my pupils. I raise my voice to end noise. I am rude to a child who is impolite, and I berate a child who uses bad language.

Dr. Haim G. Ginott

In any situation, particularly if it is one of conflict, it is essential to be careful of what you say and how you say it. Be patient, attentive, and calm. Never be condescending or trivialize the problem. Convey that you are in control of your emotions. Speak in a normal volume and deliver your message in an even cadence or rhythm. A supportive stance and relaxed bearing convey a feeling of calmness and confidence. People automatically resist when being yelled at. They go into "fight or flight" mode. The child's dignity as well as your own is not left intact when it becomes a screaming match.

Clear, Caring, and Engaged Listening

Most people do not listen with the intent to understand; they listen with the intent to reply. They're either speaking or preparing to speak. They're filtering everything through their own paradigms, reading their own autobiography into other people's lives.

Stephen R. Covey

A frequently overlooked aspect of successful behavior programs or discipline techniques is the impact of effective listening. Many conflicts can be attributed to misunderstandings or misperceptions of the intentions, feelings, needs, or actions of others. Children feel confirmed when they are truly listened to. You may not agree with your children, but you can demonstrate that you accept their feelings. You show acceptance through your tone of voice and the words you use.

Core Success Tools for You

Engaged Listening

To become an engaged listener, who hears and responds to the requests and desires of others, practice and teach clear, caring and engaged listening as follows:

- Clear Listening: Reflect back to the child what you heard her say so that she knows that you understand the meaning correctly.
- Caring Listening: Put yourself in your child's shoes in order to understand how he is feeling. You were once a child. They've not been an adult yet. Treat your child exactly the way you would like to be, or wished you as a child had been, treated.
- Engaged Listening: Always be there for the child. Try not to forget items of importance to the child. One strong positive imprint you can make on children is to recognize and make mention of their interests or accomplishments outside the home or in areas of their life in which you are not involved in, like checking in on how a friend of theirs is doing or how a game went that you didn't attend.

Without effective communication on all levels, there is little hope of having effective discipline and effective family management. Therefore, your tools and hope of building a positive, quality home climate of CORE Success lie within your own control.

Nurturing Home Climate

The importance of creating a home climate where everyone feels safe, accepted, and nurtured cannot be overstated. The essentials include:

- Trust in oneself and in and among family members.
- Sincere care and support of the individual.
- Effective communication between adults and children, and between children, is practiced.
- Children are accepted as they are and valued as complete and equal human beings.

- Children are treated with respect and dignity (and so are the adults).
- There is a cooperative living and working environment.
- Situations are set up for children so that they can succeed.
- Children are encouraged to be happy and relaxed.
- Children learn effective ways of dealing with and expressing emotion.
- Children learn conflict resolution skills—knowing how to deal with conflict creatively, fairly, and peacefully.
- Children know that they will be treated with fairness.

Having these essentials in place will certainly help to prevent and/or reduce conflict among family members, as well as making disciplining an easier task. (See activity Growing in Responsibility.)

Skills and Expectations

While establishing effective discipline methods you must understand that the skills children need to become respectful, cooperative, and responsible adults must be taught and consistently practiced until they become habit—that is, until it is an automatic response. You cannot assume that they know these skills. None of us is born knowing the very basic skills of appropriate social behavior. They must be taught at home in the early years when it is most beneficial. Also it cannot be assumed that children will learn skills of appropriate behavior from personal experience, especially given the circumstances in most youth social situations. So, it is up to us to teach the necessary skills for children to be respectful and responsible individuals.

These skills include:

- How to work and play well with each other.
- How to resolve conflict peacefully.
- How to set personal goals.
- How to manage time and organize tasks.
- The development of self-discipline.

Teaching these skills takes patience and determination, which means lots of repetition! These skills develop over many years and

> *The skills children need to become respectful, cooperative, and responsible adults must be taught until they become an automatic response (habit!).*

continue to grow into adulthood. The learning never stops.

Kids and adults alike must be willing to comply with certain rules and limits, whether it be for driving cars, following the rules of the law, respecting each other's property, paying our taxes, or following rules and respecting authority in the workplace. This is the structure that allows people to live and work together while feeling safe and secure. So it's your job to set very clear limits and rules, and to make children aware of, and be helped to understand fully, what these rules are, whether they are at home, at school, in a restaurant, on the sports field, in the school bus, etc. There must be no doubt in their minds as to what is expected of them.

The skills children need to become respectful, cooperative, and responsible adults must be taught until they become an automatic response (habit!).

Limits are the outer extent of what you are willing to tolerate. You have limits on your personal space, your emotional well-being, your work environment, and so forth. Learning to set these limits, or boundaries as they are often called, is vital for a healthy functioning sense of self. There is no room for others to choose when it comes to your limits. The same goes for the limits set for safety and well-being at home. There are no deals, there's no bargaining, or negotiations of any kind.

For example:

- "Fighting is <u>not</u> permitted."
- "No throwing inside."
- "That is disrespectful, we do <u>not</u> use those words in our home."

First create together a Family Code of Conduct based on the mission statement of your family (see the activity Our Family's Mission is... in Chapter 3, *Living to Thrive*). The Family Code of Conduct is the assurance that the values and mission your family has established will be lived and strengthened. It states clearly how everyone in the family will conduct themselves, how all want to be treated, and in what kind of environment each person wants to live. That Code of Conduct must be very specific, creating specific rules *and* behaviors that will help you achieve or maintain your family's values and mission.

In the Code of Conduct, family rules must be clearly written and parents must speak the rules every day. Rules need to be enforced. Consistency is the key. Many behaviors that you want to create must be taught and practiced so that the behavior becomes a habit or automated response. Some of the behaviors/habits formed through training and practice may seem small but are crucial in building effective discipline.

Behavior is controlled by you; you are not controlled by behavior.

Examples

You were trained very young to put on your seat belt when you got into the car. It's a habit—you don't think about it, you just do it. There are many such behaviors that are automatic, but are critical for safety and harmony in society. Stopping at a red light when driving, closing your mouth when eating, and shaking hands when you introduce yourself are all behaviors that were once foreign to you, but you were taught them and, now, don't even think twice when performing them.

The very same is true of positive conduct that adheres to the rules in your home and family. There are many behaviors that should be habit and automatic, but are not. Such behaviors include: not throwing things in the house, cleaning up after one's self at mealtime, using manners, not interrupting others, closing the door quietly, not interrupting, speaking quietly when someone else is on the phone, keeping common spaces tidy, respect for one's own belongings as well as those of others, etc.

Sandy, a teacher in one of our CORE Success for Educators Training, who taught students ages 13–16, shared this story: Sandy said that the majority of her students would let the door slam when entering or leaving the classroom, not even thinking to open or close it quietly so as not to disturb or startle anyone. She would, of course, ask them to do so quietly, but to no avail. They just weren't in the habit and would forget. So, after working through the segment on

Discipline & Decisions, she decided to go back to basics and teach them the proper way to open and close a door. Sandy demonstrated exactly how to close a door quietly. She then got several students to demonstrate as well. Every time someone came in or out and let the door slam, she had them go back to the door, and open or close the door the desired way. Eventually, the students opened and closed the door quietly most of the time. This behavior had become habit—a desirable habit replaced an undesirable one.

Here's an example from home: Telling my son that he had to clean up his room at least once a week so that we did not get bugs in the house (we were living in the woods at the time) helped little. The floor in his room was not visible beneath the piles of clothes, books, shoes, and sports equipment. So, I decided that on Sunday night everything would be put into a bag so the room could be vacuumed on Monday morning. Sunday night I gave him huge trash bags and asked him to fill them. He could re-dump them on Tuesday, but the floor was going to be cleaned. The first few times he thought it was a joke. By the end of the month, when I handed him the trash bags on Sunday night he said, "Forget it. I may as well just clean it up." And, so he did, every Sunday thereafter (with reminders, of course).

Consistency and patience are key factors.

Remember that learning new behaviors takes time. For any behavior to become a habit, or a nonthinking response, it takes repetition, repetition, and more repetition. It is said that 6 weeks are necessary to completely break an old, or train a new, habit, with 3 weeks of consistent use being the minimum.

Teaching Responsible Behavior

My son came home one day from school very disconcerted. In asking what had happened, he explained that he had done something very wrong and, in his 6-year-old opinion, "totally stupid." After assuring him that I was there to support him and help him take responsibility for his actions, he told me that he and a group of other students had broken a glass door at school. When they found a door locked that was usually open, the group began kicking the door in order to gain the attention of the teacher behind the door and down the hall. As group dynamics go, the kicking became a game and soon the intensity was such that the door shattered. In retrospect, for my son especially, this was clearly a stupid way of getting the teacher's attention. We called the principal immediately to offer our financial reimbursement, which our son contributed to, and he agreed to help replace the door if he would be allowed to. Taking responsibility for mistakes is key to learning the connection between one's own behavior, the results thereof, and the work involved in reparation.

Help children be aware that it is their home, too, and everyone has a hand and responsibility in making it a safe and happy one. Give ownership to younger and older—they must help each other behave appropriately.

Good examples and role modeling by parents is critical. Children do not magically learn kindness, respect, and self-discipline any more than they magically learn math or English. They mature into responsible adults not only by being taught the necessary skills, but also by emulating adults who are role models for them. Modeling is an important way of preventing problems. You must "walk your talk." Remember, if you prevent problems you won't have to worry about how to handle or respond to them.

Children do not magically learn kindness, respect, and self-discipline any more than they magically learn math or English.

> *Children do not magically learn kindness, respect, and self-discipline any more than they magically learn math or English.*

Misbehaving

Children don't misbehave because they are bad people. They have very good reasons for doing what they do. Finding out those reasons is immensely helpful in teaching children how to make choices that serve them and others best.

To help clarify the reasons for misbehavior, it is useful to identify a few of the categories for misbehavior. Then, using curious, nonjudgmental questions, asking your children to reflect on and explain what the reason was for their behavior (1) will go a very long way in applying logical consequences that will help them learn a better way to take care of their needs, and (2) will allow you an insight into how your children operate, thus enabling you to parent more proactively.

Children usually misbehave for one of the following reasons:

- Attention seeking
- Power seeking, revenge seeking
- Feeling of inadequacy (low self-esteem)

Let's look at them in more detail.

Attention Seeking

The underlying belief: "I only count when people are paying attention to me."

There may be many reasons for children seeking attention. It often stems from low self-esteem and a feeling of inadequacy. It may stem from a lack of maturity. The child may get little or not enough attention from loved ones, friends, or respected authority figures. They may have no or few friends; he may be accustomed to getting too much attention; she may feel the only way to be accepted and valued by adults and peers is when people pay attention to her. They seek attention to appear "cool" in front of their friends.

When we are comfortable within ourselves, when we have no fear about our circumstances, then we can be open, engaged and contribute positively to the collective. When we are not comfortable, chaos reigns - both inside and out.

Core Success Tools for You

Attention Seekers

Here are some strategies to help change attention seeking behavior.

Ignore the behavior whenever possible. If it can't be ignored, play it down—meaning, deal with it but give it the minimum amount of attention necessary. For example, if your child is throwing a fit at the clothing store, speak with your child calmly. If he/she does not calm down, return to the car and home as swiftly as possible with as little discussion as possible.

Minimize the behavior by making eye contact, standing near the child, mentioning the child's name while talking, using signals like a hand on the shoulder, speaking quietly to the child when alone, etc.

Do the unexpected by asking a direct question or asking for the child's help. Diverting attention and having the child positively engaged helps the child feel seen and useful.

Encourage appropriate behavior by giving attention when it is not needed, acknowledging the child when he/she is behaving well and cooperatively.

Develop a plan/contract with the child with clear goals on how the child can turn this disruptive behavior into positive behavior. Pay attention to successes in following that plan and celebrate them with the child.

Power Seeking / Revenge Seeking

The underlying belief: "If you don't let me do what I want, you don't love me." "I am scared when I don't have control." "If I am hurt, I will hurt back. Only then can I justify my place in this world."

Many of the reasons for attention seeking are also the reasons for power seeking/revenge seeking. Such feelings include feelings of inadequacy, low self-esteem, feeling lack of control/power in one's own life, wanting to be accepted and valued, etc. Is there a possibility of neglect or abuse at home, or bullying/abuse going on outside the home? The child may feel angry about events they suffer under and want not only power, but revenge. Experiencing bullying type behaviors puts a child into a powerless situation. Children need to know and feel that they can have some influence with people and events. They need to feel empowered and that they are in control of at least important parts of their life. However, in seeking that control, many times they tend to "press other people's buttons." Therefore, they need help in developing an internal sense of control. They need help in developing positive ways of feeling in control of themselves and their life. Address circumstances that may be at the source of this kind of behavior. If circumstances have already been addressed, here's one way to turn this behavior around:

Core Success Tools for You

Power Seekers

Sometimes power seeking behaviors can become hostile or violent. Therefore, early intervention and establishing a concrete behavior plan with your child would be wise in order to deal with the situation before it gets out of hand or someone gets hurt.

Some things that you may want to try to help change these behaviors are:

- Minimize your role as an authority figure in the scene.
- Acknowledge the child's power. Give the child something to be in charge of: making the dessert, helping a sibling get dressed, packing the car, etc.
- Redirect the conversation. For example, agree with your child on a point. This is not acquiescing but simply not engaging in a tug-of-war of who's in power.
- Set a time for later to discuss the situation. (See Appendix: What happened is...):
- Take time out for one or both parties to cool down. This should be in an appropriate area (in another room, on the porch, etc.).
- Create a Calm Down Area where children, or parents, who become irritated can go to center themselves. This area can contain some calming tools, such as, a small stereo with headphones and calming music, a squeeze toy/ball used for stress release, paper and colored pencils for writing or illustrating how the child feels, modeling clay, etc.
- Written behavior plans to turn this behavior around and help the child develop desired behaviors.
- Firm consequences to be implemented.
- Counseling from a trusted professional.
- Follow-up and evaluation of behavior plans. (Use "What happened is..." sheet as your base for improvement and need for help.)

Feeling of Inadequacy

The underlying belief: "I will not stretch to my limits as I might make mistakes. By not stretching, I avoid criticism and appear to not need help. That feels safer."

This is often the root of much unacceptable, and even bullying, behavior. For whatever reasons, the child has little confidence and low self-esteem. They may be the youngest or middle child in the family. As the oldest, they may feel they can't meet the expectations. At school they may be struggling and feel that they are "stupid." They may be used to being put down by adults and peers, or feel like they are less than a successful sibling. For whatever reason, they feel like they are a failure. Therefore, it is our job to help them build a positive self-image, to help build their confidence and self-esteem.

Core Success Tools for You

Feeling Inadequate

Here are some strategies and help for children who act out from a feeling of inadequacy.

- Accentuate the different talents and gifts of each sibling, family member.
- Speak with her teacher and ask to modify the curriculum for your child.
- Encourage and model positive self-talk.
- Give the child tasks that he can accomplish successfully.
- Talk about mistakes as necessary for the learning experience.
- Make light of your own mistakes.
- Equate mistakes with having made an effort.
- Seek assistance from other trusted adults.
- Build confidence by focusing on improvement, building on strengths, setting time limits on tasks, stressing effort made, and acknowledging accomplishments at home and at school.
- Celebrate successes.

Using these tools for misbehavior that has at its roots attention seeking, power seeking, or a sense of inadequacy will help re-train these behaviors. Gong further to create an atmosphere at home where cooperative discipline is easy to maintain is paramount to sustain positive behavior and personal core success.

Core Success Tools for You

Disciplined Home Environment

To create and maintain a quality, safe, and disciplined home environment you must:

- Help to set the tone for the day by waking up your children in a loving, calm way. Take extra time to assess the mood of your child who has challenges, therefore helping him have a good start to the day.
- Show your children, each of them, that you understand and accept them, and not only when they are successful, or when they are having difficulty.
- Encourage and motivate them.
- Help to develop individual talents and strengths.
- Focus on effort as well as achievement (since achievement can often fall short of the effort made).
- Be persistent and consistent.
- Celebrate all successes, no matter how small.

Turning Behavior Around

Children do not magically learn morality, kindness and decency any more than they learn math, English or science.

NEIL KURSHAN

It has been stated that for discipline to be effective it must be proactive not reactive. Children must know what they have done is not desired and accept ownership and responsibility for their actions. Children must decide on ways to solve problems they have created by their actions, and how they can make restitution. They must learn how to behave in different ways—in positive ways—by learning from their experience.

Core Success Tools for You

Turning Behavior Around

Formulating a plan for appropriate behavior:
Work with the child to develop an action plan for improved behavior. A plan/contract can be devised using the following steps (see Appendix: What happened is…):

- Ask questions about what happened, how the child felt, and what was unacceptable.
- The focus is on the what, when, and how of the behavior.
- Focus mainly on the present and the future.
- Write the plan down and provide the child with a copy.
- Involve other family members, teachers, and others outside the family as required.

Once the plan is formulated and written down, ask the child to make a commitment to the plan (child should say "I will do it" rather than "I will try to do it"). Children can sign the plan if desired.

Follow-up and assess how well the plan is working. Give an adequate time frame. If the plan fails, ask the child not to make excuses. Instead, make a new plan and continue the process. Celebrate successes.

Prevention

Effective cooperative discipline is proactive and a great part of being proactive is prevention. Every minute that is spent preventing problems saves considerable time spent when one has to intervene after the fact. Prevention is the best solution. This has been the underlying theme in much of what has been stated in CORE Success for Parents up to now.

"The secret to being an emotionally intelligent parent lay in how parents interacted with their children when emotions ran hot."

DR. JOHN GOTTMAN

Core Success Tools for You

Preventing Problems

Some additional and specific ideas that will help prevent problems at home are:

- Make sure that children are engaged in some activity. Self-created ones are best.
- Anticipate problems. Be aware of what may occur and prepare so they won't occur, such as, if your kids misbehave when tired, be sure sleep times are adhered to.
- Children who have difficulty in unstructured activities—such as free play—need ideas to help them stay on track. If they are doing the laundry, have them gather all socks and make sock pair balls. If cooking, have them clean the fruit. If working in the garden, have them pick up sticks. Telling a child to "Help" is not as useful as, "Please take this over there and put it in that."
- Help them decide ahead of time:
  - What game/activity they will play?
  - Who will they be with during a certain activity or event (if going on a trip, plan their activities for the trip ahead of time)?
  - Forewarn children that activities will change by giving them a "5 minutes left" notice.
- Break large chunks of work into smaller units for children who find it difficult to stay on task or who get overwhelmed easily by the whole activity, such as, "Rake the leaves around the tree first, then come see me."
- Make sure kids understand instructions. Have children who have difficulty listening and comprehending directions repeat the directions to you.
- When you notice children becoming restless, plan for a change of activities before any problems start.
- Change rules that don't work and communicate the change clearly to the whole family.

Rights and Responsibilities

With every privilege that one has, one has an accompanying responsibility. If a child has the right to find her things in their place and in order, she also has the responsibility to care for others' belongings and return them to their appropriate place. If a child has the right to be spoken to respectfully, he has the responsibility of practicing respectful language with others. Understanding this two-sided coin helps children willingly train their behavior, knowing that all parties, themselves included, profit from it. (See activity Rights and Responsibility.)

Reliability is a trait that has been lost by the wayside. As parents you can emphasize its importance and point it out when your children practice it, and when you provide it. Keeping one's word is like one's personal signature of behavior and integrity. Integrating into family time and activities the idea of reliability and keeping one's word will greatly aid children in training self-discipline. These attributes are sought in the workplace, and in healthy relationships, and will benefit children now and for their future.

Respect

In the sandboxes of today, children are taught that the bucket and shovel found there are not theirs. Their toys are in *this* bag and one should always ask before taking, and share when others would like to play. This is, of course, teaching rules of our social behavior. However, the idea of "mine and yours" has many and far reaching results. If not done consciously one of the results is the belief that "I need only to care for those items that belong to me." Caring for one's self and one's own things is the first step to respect. The rest of the story is to respect as well, and equally, others, and the items that belong to them.

We must teach our children that responsibility reaches beyond their own small circle of interest to the world around them. This doesn't mean that they police each other, but that they increase their awareness of what goes on around them. As one teacher in our educator's training wrote to her class after a very disturbing bout of vandalism: "You are not only responsible for what you do, but also for what you do not do. It is not a question of whether one student destroys or bullies another student, but rather that each person feels responsible to assure the rules are kept and people are safe. If the person who breaks the rule is not in a position to take responsibility, then someone else should take the responsibility to do something about it, i.e. encourage the person to act appropriately or to inform a an adult."

Setting Goals

Often channeling the incredible energies of children will help tremendously when working with issues of discipline. One very effective tool is goal setting. When given the opportunity to focus their creative potential, ideas and desires in a certain direction and then given the time, tools, and motivation to follow that path, a lot of nonsensical or disruptive behavior will simply fall away. Goal setting is a tool that develops logical and consequential thinking, creates positive self-motivation, and adds to the foundation for leadership. It is an extremely important aspect of supporting children, especially older children and teenagers.

You can view your goals in life as locations on a map. First you must know where you are in order to know how to get to where you are going. It is not possible to get to Rome unless you first establish where you are on the globe! It will make a huge difference in plotting your journey, whether your current location is Bangkok or Denver! Since you are the one living your life, it is important that this map is one that you have designed, know intimately, and can navigate and change at will, if necessary.

Use goal setting for daily tasks, like setting an agenda for homework and for long-term planning of dreams. With clarity, a game plan, and work, you can achieve the goals you set. Your attitude and sense of self are key in achieving what you desire. Goals are dealt with in more depth in *The CORE Success Discipline Guide for Parents*.

Conclusion

Life is very busy and seems to be getting busier by the day. There is never enough time to accomplish all the things you are asked to or want to do. However, effective discipline takes time, patience, persistence, and consistency. The time investment, however, is so phenomenally worth it in the long run, saving endless hours of arguments, behavioral issues, and even worry once the kids have left home. But mostly, people feel better, are happier, and healthy relationships get stronger. You must fully realize you are the authority, the captain of the ship. Without the captain, there's no direction. Without the crew, the ship gets nowhere. You must take charge, make the decisions that need to be made, set limits that need to be set, and know when to allow your children to make their own decisions.

A family Code of Conduct (based on the mission statement) with clear, precise rules stated and possible consequences discussed must be developed together in the family, then be put into writing and discussed often in the family.

Most important of all, parents must live CORE Success themselves: Clarity, Ownership, Resolution, and Excellence. You must always remember that whatever you do, you must leave your dignity and that of your children intact. When parents and children make the commitment to establishing cooperative discipline and creating a peaceful, supportive home environment, they can then say goodbye to chaos. Your children are gifts. Some come in very unique packaging, yet they are all special gifts and must be treated as gifts. Make the commitment and use the tools to encourage and teach them to become all they can be. They are the *future* so give them the tools to create a positive one.

CORE Success Factors of Discipline with Dignity

CLARITY	OWNERSHIP	RESOLUTION	EXCELLENCE
Define what discipline is Set discipline expectations	Practice cooperative discipline Establish rules and consequences 3 Rs: respect for self, respect for others, responsibility Cooperation Turn behavior around	Consequences not punishment Use clear listening Change attention, power, and revenge seeking behaviors Diffuse conflict Define rights and responsibility	Make rules and consequences Build connected relationship Communicate well Prioritize positive home environment Empower kids Be proactive, prevent problems Commit

Keys to CORE Success

⚡ Rules and limits are never negotiable, consequences can be.

⚡ Manage the problem, love the person.

⚡ Observe and describe the facts; don't judge.

⚡ Ask questions, and believe the answers.

⚡ Communicate clearly, addressing the child's behavior while preserving the child's dignity, as well as your own.

⚡ For discipline to be effective it must be proactive not reactive.

⚡ Always be firm, fair, kind, and consistent.

⚡ Seek to understand the reasons for misbehavior.

⚡ Children do not magically learn kindness, respect, and self-discipline. You are the teacher.

⚡ Prioritize connecting, want to understand.

⚡ Ask yourself: What do I want? How can I best get there?

⚡ Plan ahead.

⚡ Focus on one issue at a time.

⚡ Be a respectful captain.

⚡ Motivate with happiness.

⚡ Communicate authentically.

⚡ Believe in good! They're doing their best given their current understanding and abilities.

⚡ Use the CORE Success tools.

Challenges and FAQs

✓ *Discipline is such a big issue that I really don't know where to start.* Start with establishing a code of conduct. You can do this by first deciding on the nonnegotiable rules, rights, and responsibilities you and your partner hold for your family. With that in mind, during a family meeting, create your code of conduct. Let the kids lead this. Write it down and post it somewhere. Then you can also discuss the consequences for possible infringements. Again, have the kids be involved in this step as well, although you will be the decider of consequences when there is an infringement.

✓ *The misbehavior just baffles me. How can I turn that around for good?* First, remember that it is a process! Improvement happens in spurts and stops and can be all over the map. Second, find out the reason for the misbehavior. If there is consistent lying, then either there is a trust issue, the child is involved in something that she wants to hide, or communication needs to be focused on. If the child is consistently aggressive, find out the triggers, what the child is thinking and feeling, if there are other causes (e.g., dietary, environmental, or bullying issues taking place). Once you have found the causes, work through the Turning Behavior Around worksheet in the Appendix.

✓ *I get that blaming is counterproductive, but I have no clue what else to do when things go south.* Awareness is the first step. It's so important to first notice the blame and then to identify that it is not helpful. And therein lies your answer. When an issue occurs, a conflict arises, ask yourself, "What would be helpful here?" For example, if you hear a crash, rush into the living room, and find your vase with flowers broken on the carpet, the most helpful thing would be to get the garbage pail for the remnants and glass and towels for the water. After that has been taken care of, asking questions as to what took place, is the next step. When you figure out they were playing football in the living room (against house rules), you can engage the kids in the discipline process. Why were they playing inside and against house rules? What do they think should be done to make amends (use pocket money to buy a new vase, etc.)?

ANCHOR WITH ACTIVITIES

Rights and Responsibilities

What's the point?

To develop an understanding of what a *right* is and what a *responsibility* is. To develop an understanding that for every right there is a corresponding responsibility.

What do I need?

Chart paper, pencils/markers, CORE Success Notebook, see Appendix: Rights and Responsibilities

What do I do?

Write the title "Right" on one piece of chart paper. Write the title "Responsibility" on another piece of chart paper. Ask children to write what they think a right is in their P.E.A.C.E. Notebook. They can write a word or definition, or just write words or phrases that come to mind.

Together make a list of their current rights at home on chart paper, such as have meals, go to school, sleep in a bed, etc. Follow the same procedure for the second term, responsibility, such as help set the table, do my homework, change my sheets, etc.

Note: Definitions:

Right: Privilege, or just claim.

Responsibility: Something for which you are responsible; an obligation; duty; what one is expected to do.

Take it a step further

Create a list of Rights and Responsibilities for your family. Using list already formed can be a springboard for this.

How do I continue the conversation?

Questions for discussion:

- Why should you have rights?
- Why do you have responsibilities/rules?
- What is the correlation between rights and responsibilities?
- What happens if you have one without the other, or if they are not in balance?
- Can you think of another name for Rights (gifts)? Responsibilities (rules)?
- Can you select one of these rights that has been listed and pair it up with a responsibility that has been written on the chart?

Cooperative Rule Making

What's the point?

To increase awareness of what cooperative rule making is and the importance of it. To empower children so they feel ownership of their home and feel a part of the family by allowing them to be part of the development of family rules.

Note: Involving children as rule makers may take more time, but it is a worthwhile investment because:

- Children help define the standards.
- They have more interest in making the rules work.
- They become more involved in monitoring each other's behavior.
- They have more opportunity to become responsible.
- They learn and apply problem-solving skills.

What do I need?

Chart paper, markers/pencils, CORE Success Notebook, see Appendix: Criteria for a Good Rule

What do I do?

Review the importance of rules and why people need them. Share the sheet *Criteria for a Good Rule* and discuss what a good rule is. Ask children for examples of good rules and bad rules. You can use rules from home, school, society, etc.

Ask children to develop three rules for the family/home that meet the criteria of a good rule and record in CORE Success Notebook. Once they have three rules, then have children devise a role play that could demonstrate what one rule would look like when it is broken thus showing the importance of rules and why we need them.

Take it a step further

Together create some rules for the family that will then be recorded as a Family Code of Conduct. Sometimes one main rule may be used as a Golden Rule, but with specifics listed below. How do these rules relate to our list of rights and responsibilities? Post this Code somewhere in a prominent place in the home.

How do I continue the conversation?

- Are these good rules? Why or why not?
- Are they important?
- Why does our family need these rules?
- Why is our family deciding these rules together?

Here would be a good opportunity to discuss the spirit of cooperation: This is our home and we are all responsible for what happens here. There are many choices and decisions we need to make daily, such as which jobs each of us will do, how we respond to each other, what we can and cannot do when we feel upset or angry. We each have the right to be in a safe, respectful, supportive, caring, and positive learning environment, but we each have the responsibility to help create and maintain such a great home climate.

CHAPTER 6

Resolving Conflict

*We must find an alternative to violence. This eye
for an eye philosophy leaves everybody blind.*

MARTIN LUTHER KING JR.

Conflict is a natural occurrence in our daily lives. Conflict
occurs when differing opinions or desires collide and a
seemingly unresolvable situation results. Usually, conflicts
involve two or more people, or even groups of people. (Heck, even
when there's only one person involved, namely ourselves, we can
have conflict!) That's a part of life—different cultures, different
opinions, different wants.

The Core Point ... and Your Gain

Conflict itself is not the problem; it's rather how you deal with
conflict that is. It becomes a problem when the conflict disturbs
your ease and well-being, your relationships and effectiveness,

when you are unable to resolve it in a peaceable and fair manner for all involved. That's what we explore here: how you can engage in the natural conflicts that occur in a way that is respectful and yet can create solutions that allow all parties to be heard and a common solution to be found.

Simple misunderstanding as well as more serious disputes, based on differences of opinions, beliefs, needs, goals, traditions, personal history, etc. can often lead to friction and conflict. Conflict is acceptable; violence—verbal, emotional, physical, or otherwise—is not. Headlines continually point out the terrible reality that our society, on the whole, is unable to solve conflicts fairly and peaceably. The most alarming fact, however, is that our youth have come to believe that conflict is a reason, even permission, for violence, acts of aggression, and even revenge, which are seen as acceptable forms of resolving conflict. Understanding, resolution, and working together are not traits that, as a rule, are actively being taught to our youth. And this trend continues to spiral out of control. Home is an optimal place to turn the tide—a place kids feel connected and empowered to learn positive conflict resolution skills.

The ideas and tools of *Resolving Conflict* are empathy, mastering feelings, engaged listening and effective communication skills, eradicating blame, dealing with conflict, and conflict resolution skills. Studying these basics, and practicing them daily at home, even using role-plays and skits, will give everyone, especially kids, the ability to deal well with conflicts as they arise.

Conflict is acceptable; violence — verbal, emotional, physical, or otherwise — is not.

External vs. Internal Orientation

Conflict resolution and violence prevention begins with awareness. Learning how to read situations, to differentiate what goes on out there in the world at large, and in here (within yourself) is vital to conflict resolution. Awareness of your feelings and your behavior, and those of others, is key to utilizing the steps to solve problems. Self-studentship is a valuable tool to raise your awareness and increase your capacity to apply the steps of conflict resolution.

When you become a student of yourself, your focus is not self-centered but self-directed. By being aware of your own thoughts, desires, and needs you learn to be more present. Instead of comparing yourself to others, you can build a strong

> **Conflict is acceptable; violence — verbal, emotional, physical, or otherwise — is not.**

sense of self-acceptance and trust that work as an internal navigation system showing you how to maneuver through the events of your day. Since you are the one living your life, it is important that this roadmap is one that you have self-designed, know intimately, can navigate, or can change at will. Learning to trust your own assessment and take self-directed action is a process in which you can practically support your children. Dynamic trust in yourself is trust that is constantly challenged, questioned, confirmed, and relied upon on a daily basis. Self-awareness and self-studentship can be learned.

You are constantly screening everything that happens. Each and every event in your daily life—big or small—either pleases you, doesn't please you, or is elevator music (as neurobiologist Bruce Lipton says)—meaning, you don't really care about it either way. Roughly stated, you evaluate the world according to this simple formula: Will this benefit me or not? You divide events generally into these two groups and act based upon this compartmentalization. If my worldview is that what happens out there (meaning the world outside myself) determines largely how I feel and live, then I need to focus a lot of my energies on changing the out there factor. This proves to be a very time and energy consuming, not to mention futile, exercise. The answer is to master the in here factor, master yourself.

Often we are only vaguely aware of our relationships and the situations we find ourselves in. Practicing clear awareness gives us connection to our own power in any situation. Combine that clear awareness with an understanding for yourself that it is not what happens but *how you feel* about what's going on that determines your life and your well-being—then you've put yourself into the driver's seat. You can train and implement language and behavior for yourself that expresses that you are in charge of *your* own world, no matter what takes place out there. Then, you can interact with people and events out there from a seat of strength in yourself, while not making others responsible for how you feel and act. You can communicate what is going on in here (inside yourself) and state your needs and take decisive action without making anyone else wrong in order to do so.

Core Success Tools for You

External vs. Internal Orientation

By training a clear awareness of yourself, and of situations you are in, you will learn to respond to people and situations in a self-confirming and constructive manner. Differentiating "external" and "internal" orientation increases your ability to:

- Recognize your own feelings
- Recognize and understanding another's feelings
- See your available choices—when and how to respond
- Make behavioral decisions that serve both yourself and others

You can increase awareness and differentiated behavior by practicing the following skills:

- Active and engaged listening
- Using clear and accurate communication—"I Messages"
- Dealing nonjudgmentally—not making others wrong; using observation instead of value judgment
- Expressing feelings in an assertive and self-responsible manner
- Using concrete problem-solving steps

For example:

Someone cuts in front of you while you are waiting in a long line for a new blockbuster movie.

	Reactive External Awareness	Clear Internal Awareness
Awareness	Huh? That's uncool!	She came from the back of the line.
	She is so toast. She better move it!	I wonder why she's stepping into the middle of the line.
Feeling	NOT fair! Anger.	I'm irritated. I've been waiting here for 15 minutes.
Choices	Push her out; yell	Let her stay there; point it out: insist she leave
Response	Yell	I'll tell her it's not okay to cut in, and see what happens.
Outcome	She left. I was right.	I told her we're all waiting and would she go to the end of the line. I feel good.
Conclusion	Only aggression, anger get me what I want.	No outside trigger decides my behavior: I alone decide.

Using this awareness and developing it through use of guidelines and skills for conflict resolution will train children and adults to analyze, respond to, and resolve conflict in a humane and empowering manner.

Empathy

Often knowing how you feel is a challenge in itself. Going beyond that to understand how others are feeling by putting yourself in their shoes to see the world from their particular viewpoint is a valuable skill. It is a skill that can be practiced, and imparted to others— namely, your kids. Developing the ability to understand others from their frame of reference, sometimes referred to as empathy, is not a given and yet can be acquired at any age, the earlier the better. Adult criminals who were bullies in their youth are characterized by an inability to empathize with what another person is feeling. They live in their own isolated world of intense feelings, not possessing the insight into how others around them may feel. When empathy is taught and practiced on a regular basis, the rate of bullying, aggression, and violence at schools drastically decreases (Cierpka, 1997). Knowing your feelings, active and engaged listening, I Messages, and removing blame are the key elements for developing empathy.

Core Success Tools for You

Empathy

First of all, be aware that all behavior has a motivating force behind it. When you see your child behaving a certain way, actually look for the motivator behind the behavior. With practice, you'll get pretty good at identifying it. Asking directly and with a sense of curiosity often works well, especially with younger children, such as, Why did you throw the ball at his head? A child is not randomly being cruel because of his true nature. A child is acting out because he believes not to have any other alternatives to getting what he wants or has not yet developed skills in positive social behavior to act accordingly. How does knowing this help parents? It gives insight into the drive behind the behavior.

So, instead of reacting out of your sense of disappointment and anger at the apparent lack of love between siblings, you can act from a place of understanding and firmness. Understanding where another person is at, and knowing what you yourself want, gives you the power to choose how you want to act in any given situation. You can also use your understanding to speak out the situation for the siblings. Even if they don't admit it, or work it out, they are absolutely learning from you sharing different ways to view situations from perspectives other than their own.

Few of us live in communities where kids of varying ages are available to meet the diverging needs of developing children. Hence, similar sibling conflicts arise daily. It is helpful to:

- Train communication skills, such as I Messages and active and engaged listening.
- Make the children aware of their different needs through discussions and naming (speaking it out for children who cannot yet express it for themselves).
- Help them listen to each other in order to develop empathy—the understanding of how another person is feeling.
- Teach them to seek solutions in which all parties are considered and respected.
- Participate in the solution finding process until they can master it on their own. (See activity Talking Stick Untangler, at the end of this chapter.)

Freedom of Feelings

Feelings are the emotional expression of what you sense from, and think about, yourselves, others, and the interactions with the world. Your feelings are learned directly, or indirectly, from your personal experiences and from input from the world around you. Being clear about one's own feelings not only leads to a positive sense of self, it is vital to effective communication and conflict resolution. Being aware that you own your emotions instead of having them own you is a key to maturity. Understanding what you are feeling, and being sure that you are not the victim of your emotions, leads you to a solid, healthy, assertive way of living your life.

For example, when a child is overwhelmed because, being the smallest in the group, he is often excluded, overlooked, and made fun of, it can be helpful to examine the variety of feelings going on inside of him. He may be sad and angry, or he may feel helpless. Hopefully, he is able to name those feelings about his experiences. Offering him the opportunity to say that he feels like he is not good enough because he is smaller than the others, or that he feels disliked because he is different, helps him name the shadows that may haunt him. It is also then a good starting point to discuss differences in your bodies and appearances. Look at the differences each person has in size, coloring, weight, and abilities. Gently teach the child to see her feelings about her size as something she can change (the feelings, not the size) with practice and support.

Knowing your intrinsic worth will lead you to accepting yourself and, hence, to dealing better with challenging or opposing input from others. Knowing your feelings, exploring them, confirming or altering them through conviction, and strengthening your feelings of innate rightness will all contribute to your healthy self-esteem and to strong and healthy connections with others. This is the key to dealing well with conflict.

In order to understand how others feel, you must first understand your own feelings. (More activities for dealing with feelings can be found in the CORE Success for Parents Activity Guide.) Then the step to understanding others is an easier one, especially if practiced using active listening and understanding, and suspending judgment and blame.

Engaged Listening and Understanding

Training skills to listen with attentiveness and nonjudgment is paramount to effective problem solving. When you can be free to really hear what the other persons is saying, hear their reasoning and background, then understanding and empathy can surface. Practicing the following skills will be helpful.

Engaged listening, or active listening as it is often referred to, means being fully engaged in the listening process, not in talking or formulating a response. You use certain tools to hear what another person is sharing. There are very clear markers that identify active listening. It is one of the most powerful skills you can develop, and definitely a key one for resolving conflict.

"To effectively communicate, we must realize that we are all different in the way we perceive the world and use this understanding as a guide to our communication with others."

TONY ROBBINS

Core Success Tools for You

Engaged Listening and Understanding

Remind the children (or better yet, role model it!) to use engaged and active listening, especially while they are in conflict or resolution. Here's what you can practice even without conflict … just to get good!

Engaged listening behaviors:

- Use eye contact while speaking.
- Indicate you are listening, perhaps by nodding your head, or saying a word or two to indicate you are listening, such as, oh; I see; really?
- Listen without formulating your own response.
- Listen without judging (without labeling as wrong or right) what you are hearing.
- Wait until the speaker has finished before you respond.
- Ask questions if you are unclear about what the other person said.
- Summarize to be sure you have understood correctly.
- Think about, or ask, how the other person is feeling.

Nonlistening behaviors are, for example:

- Changing the subject or interrupting.
- Thinking about something else or formulating what you want to say.
- Turning away from or not looking at the person who is speaking.
- Ignoring or fidgeting.
- Making fun of what the person is saying.
- Making disrespectful or rude statements.
- Giving advice.
- Looking bored.

Much acclaimed author and trainer Stephen Covey speaks about the art of active listening in many of his books. He correctly distils the truth that we spend years of our lives learning to speak and hundreds of hours, in school and out, learning to read, write, and do arithmetic. But the most important skill of all, one we need and use every single day, one that leads to understanding and union or to misunderstanding and dissention, is the ability to really listen to someone else. Yet, we have had no formal training in it! Usually it is assumed that one *can* listen well. And that is where communication often breaks down—each person lost in his own interpretation of what was just said.

But the most important skill of all, one we need and use every single day, one that leads to understanding and connection or to misunderstanding and dissention, is the ability to really listen to someone else.

Yet where should the ability of active listening have been acquired? The role models most of us have had were seldom modeling this valuable skill very well, if at all. The humanistic psychologist, Dr. Carl Rogers, studied the transformational power of being deeply heard by another human being. When someone feels truly heard, understood, and accepted at a fundamental level for precisely how one feels, that being heard, that acceptance offers the speaker a healing that is both profound and simple. It is a powerful practice. (Early in my career I had the honor to interpret for and assist Dr. Natalie Rogers, Carl Rogers' daughter and colleague, for a number of years at her various person-centered art therapy trainings in Europe. That unique opportunity impacted not only me personally, but dramatically influenced my work and has served as a foundation for CORE Success.) As parents we have a wonderful opportunity to be role models for active listening, and for integrating this important learning process into our daily life. Thus, we offer children and ourselves the chance to practice true listening, whenever we are communicating with others. (See activity: Active Listening/Listen and Share Mats in this chapter.)

> **But the most important skill of all, one we need and use every single day, one that leads to understanding and connection or to misunderstanding and dissention, is the ability to really listen to someone else.**

I Messages vs. You Messages

Sharing how you feel from an authentic and respectful place goes a long way in being heard by others and in resolving challenging situations more comfortably. Marshall Rosenberg, a student of Carl Rogers, distilled Rogers' work in empathic listening into what has become known as nonviolent communication. The basics of I Messages are very simple. Using I Messages does not mean using the word "I" in every sentence. I Messages have the hallmark of expressing solely the feelings and experience of the speaker, of sharing how a person perceived and then experienced an event or another person. The comments are the sole expression of one's personal experience. "I think you're a jerk," *is not* an I Message. It is an insult. "I feel really ticked that you left during the middle of the film and didn't come back," is an I Message. It states the fact (the person left and didn't come back) and then expresses clearly the speaker's feeling about the fact (I'm ticked). No accusation involved.

1. "Every day you leave the kitchen a huge mess after you come home from school. You are so amazingly sloppy. You don't care about anyone but yourself."

2. "Hilary, when I come home from the office I'm tired and need to have just a short break from working. If the kitchen has dirty dishes in the sink and pots left on the stove I feel overwhelmed. I feel like I'm expected to clean up the mess. I would like you to clean up your own mess before I get home."

In quotes #1 and #2 the same content is being shared, but the manner and message are quite different. In #1, a You Message, there are accusations and blame involved. The dissatisfaction is being dumped from the frustrated person onto the person who left the mess. It is generalized (every day) and not specific (mess, sloppy). A natural reaction to an attack such as this would be a counterattack. The first person who comes home tired is then attacked in return, and then even more upset since she is not responsible for the mess. But she does not see the cause of the conflict escalation rooted in her #1 You Message. Therein lies the reason for most conflict and miscommunication. You Messages are destructive and threaten connection.

In #2, an I Message, the dissatisfaction is expressed clearly and fairly by the person feeling the upset, sharing specifically what happened and how she feels without making someone else wrong. At the end of the statement the desired change is requested, again without using blame or insult. This I Message will most likely be received as an expression of someone's personal dissatisfaction rather than as a personal attack. The willingness to listen and the desire to assist the speaker is much more likely. A commonly satisfying resolution to the situation is a good bet, with connection intact.

Core Success Tools for You

I Messages

I Message Format: Easy to remember, easy to use.

Observation	Say what your senses perceive	There are dirty dishes and pots in the sink and on the counter when I got home from work tonight.
Feeling	Explain your feelings honestly and transparently	After work I'm tired and I feel overwhelmed when I find the kitchen a mess.
Desire	State what's important to you, your desire/want	I would like a break from working when I get home.
Request	Request an action, a strategy, a decision	I would like you to clean up your mess when you use the kitchen.

When you speak to others you can really only share your own perception of things, your own wants, and your own understanding of a situation. It is erroneous to believe that you can accurately state what another person is feeling, has experienced, or intends. Only that person, themself, can correctly know and share that information. So, it is each person's obligation in communication to speak about what is going on for one's self in any given situation. Stating this in a manner that does not attack, but rather expresses one's own viewpoint is an effective, almost magical, way to either deescalate conflict or share dissatisfaction in a way that minimizes the chance of conflict arising. Listening to someone share, without judging her but rather with the desire to understand, is the other half of that magical equation.

The Burden of Blame

Blame is believing another person is at fault for something. Blame may or may not be expressed, but here we will deal with its expression. Blame usually instills a sense of shame in the person being blamed. Blaming escalates the situation, a push and shove of accusations results, and a solution to the problem becomes elusive. Blaming others is the flip side of taking responsibility for one's own actions—blaming does not empower either party. If each involved party would take responsibility and own the part that he played, it becomes obvious that blame is superfluous, and a solution would be more readily found. In most conflicts, however, blame imposes its heavy load and hinders resolution.

The vicious cycle of blame usually takes place when the accuser feels guilty. Sound strange? Think about it. We usually blame others when we, ourselves, feel we could perhaps be at fault or could have prevented something from happening, or we feel the need to exonerate ourselves. When someone feels guilty, feeling she has done something wrong, then that person usually blames another to alleviate the feelings of "being bad." (The belief that "I am bad" was instilled in many of us as small children. When we did something wrong we were told "you *are* a bad boy/girl.") Since no one wants to feel he "is bad" at heart, we learn not to take ownership of what we *have done* trying to retain the belief that, if we don't own up to having done it, we *are* still good. We believe that if we were to admit our actions that contributed to an event, that admission would confirm "our badness." Hence, we push the blame onto someone else to relieve ourselves of guilt. This, however, then leads to the other person's indignation and often triggers their own guilt and feeling of being "bad." It's a vicious cycle. In other words, it is paramount to remember that although a behavior could be called wrong, bad, or at least not wanted, the person who took the action is not a bad person.

Core Success Tools for You

Ban Blame and Seek Solutions

How can one get out from under this burden of blame? One simple and effective way is to stop blaming and look for solutions.

- Take responsibility for your own actions, no matter how small or inconsequential. Speak that ownership out loud to all involved.
- Involve all parties in actively seeking a solution.
- No one is blamed for the situation.
- Everyone involved is held responsible for its resolution.
- If possible, those not involved can be included in finding a solution.

This approach to solution seeking does not fit all situations, but is most effective when dealing with group problems and convoluted explanations. It is also a time-saver when you, as the adult, cannot go into other problem-solving techniques such as The Talking Stick.

Relief of Responsibility

Another way to stop blaming is to drop self-righteousness and to train taking responsibility. Both of those steps are mighty difficult for many of us. (See Chapter 5, *Discipline with Dignity.*) When you practice dropping self-righteousness and instead take ownership, you, as an adult, can model this behavior in your everyday dealings and your children learn it more easily. The need to "be right" is deeply rooted in most of us. Sometimes we are more willing to let a relationship die than to admit we were wrong. Practicing the relief of responsibility can become a skill that you first must acquire and then you can teach others, especially your children.

Core Success Tools for You

Relief of Responsibility

The next time you are at work, or at home, and something has gone wrong, just sit back and quietly but keenly observe what sequence of events take place.

- Almost always the first reaction is for a person, machine, or even God to be blamed for the event or problem.
- Then comes complaining about the situation. This may be long or short, depending on the attitude of the person with the problem.
- And at last, if even, the search for a solution or remedy begins.

In such a situation try out one of the following actions:

- Take full responsibility for the problem or situation quickly, even if you had nothing to do with it! Make this a proclamation: "Oh, I take full responsibility for that!" People will be amazed. It's a showstopper, and tension dissolver. Then see what happens ...
- And/or interrupt the blame phase by offering to find a solution: "Instead of looking for people, let's look for solutions." Make suggestions, and look for alternatives, as long as you do not get involved in the burden of blame pattern.
- Then watch how the situation evolves.

One day in the grocery store a lady's boot caught a box of cereal on the bottom shelf. With her next step the box and the whole lower shelf of cereal boxes tumbled into the aisle. The other people turned to look as the lady exclaimed, "I didn't do that." No one, including the lady, made a move to clean up the mess. A young man came from behind the crowd and said, "Oh, what a coincidence. I just wanted one of those. Here, let me help pick those up." These simple words brought immediate ease to the situation, and then all the people in the aisle bent down together to rebuild the rows of cereal boxes. He took responsibility, issued no blame, and offered to rectify the situation. It's a hoot.

Siblings and Their Rivalry

After a tussle between cousins, I asked my 13-year-old nephew, why, for Pete's sake, they fight so often. This is what he told me:

"It's not that I don't love my brother. I do. But he's a lot younger [in this case, almost 4 years] and has different interests than I do. When I'm doing something, he wants to do it too, but not because he's really interested in it. He's just not at the same place as I am. Usually he does it because I'm doing it. So then I feel like he's not doing it *with* me, but following me. That's not necessarily bad, but then I don't feel we're equal. I don't feel I'm playing *with* him. There are two different levels going on, and I don't want that all the time. I also want to just play at my own level. It feels frustrating as the older one to always have to accommodate for that difference."

When I asked him if he could say that to his brother, or deal with the situation with kindness, he said that when he tries, his brother doesn't understand or respect his desires. So, he reverts to just using his power. He knows well that he is bigger and can get what he wants through force. So he does.

That's one perspective. On the other hand, the younger child is looking up to the older child and wants to connect, to learn from, and emulate the older child (even if they are different sexes). This can be misinterpreted as clinginess or, often, as being a pest. The younger ones are also know well that they don't have the power, size, or strength the older ones do. So, in order to get what they want, they compensate for their weaker position by whining, crying, begging, tattling—it's their leverage. It usually works with us parents, because we like to jump right in if someone seems unfairly treated. As a result of our involvement, resentment builds between the two siblings and then everyone gets more frustrated.

From an adult point of view, the ways kids try to get what they want may appear ineffective. However, for children, this is the best way to accomplish their goal, which is to get their needs met. The question remains, what are parents to do in order to facilitate more harmonious relationships between siblings, and in your home? How can you foster a strong connection between siblings?

First of all, be aware that all behavior has a motivating force behind it. Children are not randomly being cruel because that is their true nature. Children are acting out because they believe that they do not have any other alternatives to getting what they want, or have not yet developed the self-discipline to practice positive social behavior. How does knowing this help you as parents? It gives you insight into the drive behind the behavior. So, instead of reacting out of your sense of disappointment and anger at the apparent lack of love between siblings, you can act from a place of understanding and firmness. Understanding where another person is at, and knowing where you yourself are, gives you the power to choose how you want to act in any given situation.

Core Success Tools for You

Removing the Rivalry

Since most families, and neighborhoods, may not have many kids of different ages to meet the needs of developing children, conflicts at home arise more often, even daily. It is helpful to:

- Train communication skills. (See activity I Messages.)
- Help kids become aware of their differing feelings and needs through discussions and naming the feelings (speaking it for children who struggle to express their feelings for themselves. Teenagers often fall into this category!).
- Help siblings listen to each other in order to develop empathy (the understanding of how another person is feeling—see activity Listen & Share Mats).
- Teach the kids to seek solutions in which all parties are considered and respected.
- As the adult, participate in the solution finding process until they can master it on their own (see activity Talking Stick Untangler).

Plan for Success: Make sure all kids have good friends and play relationships in their daily lives so they are getting their age-appropriate needs met.

Anger and Impulse Mastery

You can't shake hands with clenched fists.

INDIRA GANDHI

Violence (aggression felt inside that is turned outward) is an uncontrolled escalation of human emotion that can no longer be contained. Research shows that in order to deal effectively with violence and potential violence, a number of aspects of our human side must be addressed regularly and with insight. Considering that aggressive behavior has different motivation for each of us, depending on the people involved and the circumstances, our motivational factors must be addressed (Nolting et al., 1993). Anger is a large source of conflict and violence. Anger is not bad, but it is vital that we learn how to manage, and what to do with, our anger.

Anger is a common response to many situations. Watching young children starve, hearing of social injustice, and war being waged without being able to stop it are only a few events to which people react with anger. There is nothing wrong with anger in itself, but what you do with it is crucial. It is not acceptable to unload one's anger onto another person, or to physically or emotionally injure someone with your anger. It is your responsibility to manage your own anger when it arises, to give it a healthy path of expression, or to resolve it.

Speaking about feelings in general, anger especially, with young people will need help to identify and become more comfortable with what goes on inside of them. It will also help them see that they are not alone in their world of emotions. Getting to know your feelings helps you know yourself better, and to accept all aspects of yourself. Knowing yourself well is the key to mastering your emotions, and your life. The more you know what you feel, what you want and don't want, and where you want to go, basically just how you operate, the more you have a sense of power and of mastery over your life. This sense of mastery leads not only to less conflict, it builds self-esteem, understanding of others, and creates an inner pathway to kindness. First you are accepting of yourself and then you can be accepting of others.

Reading My Body

After learning to identify, name, and accept their feelings, children can then observe how the emotions affect their physical body. Some kids are much more in touch with their bodies; this is a great helping tool for them.

Core Success Tools for You

Reading My Body

The following questions can be asked when children are experiencing different feelings. You can also practice trying on different feelings as an exercise and ask the same questions:

- How is my breathing?
- What are my hands doing?
- How do my muscles feel?
- Am I hot, cold, or just normal?
- What thoughts are going through my head?
- What does my body feel like doing right now, such as, sitting, running, hitting…?

Triggers That Trick

Everyone has distinct buttons that evoke certain emotions. These buttons can be pushed or triggered by certain situations, statements, or even people. It is helpful for us to identify the triggers (things that happen out there in the world) that bother us and lead to our anger or other intense or uncomfortable feelings. (This is especially helpful for sensitive children or children with special needs.) With awareness and practice, we learn what our triggers are. Being prepared for things that trigger us can help us to choose our responses ahead of time and to master our feelings instead of being controlled by them.

Core Success Tools for You

Triggers That Trick

In a quiet moment have the children (and yourself) make a list of their own triggers, which they, and you, respond to with anger. Keep the list handy (in a purse, a backpack, a wallet). When something occurs and you feel angry or distressed, see if that event, the trigger, is on your list. If not, add it. If so, speak about other options of dealing with the trigger than with anger or distress.

Calming Quotients

Recognizing the physical signs of anger serves as the first step in anger management. When the signs are clear, then steps to channel the anger can be taken.

Core Success Tools for You

Calming Quotients

Some tools to use when you are angry are:

- Breathe deeply, following your breath three times in and three times out.
- Take time out, quiet and alone, to cool down. Focus on looking at something pleasant—a tree, a nice picture, a new pair of shoes.
- Think of something calming or happy.
- Count backward slowly from 10 to 1.
- Use the I Message format to speak to yourself about your current experience.

Loosening Anger's Anchor

Sometimes too much tension has built up and you need to do something to let off steam. It can feel like the anger and frustration have their hooks in you. The skill is to deal with that incredible energy without hurting yourself, or someone else, and give yourself time to become centered. Then you can deal with the situation calmly and appropriately.

Core Success Tools for You

Dealing with Anger

Here are two very effective ways of dealing with anger that has you in its grip:

Run it Off: When? After an argument, after work, after school, in the middle of a fight, as soon as possible.

A school in New York state started a "Run It Off" program. During recess a few teachers encouraged kids, whose frustration level had built up during class time, to pound it out through their feet! These kids grabbed the opportunity to run with other "angry kids" around the playground four times. It was so successful that the group decided to meet regularly to "Run It Off" for fun. The group is now an established activity during recess. It is open to all students, of any age, and the anger level has dropped dramatically for these kids. This is more proof that the conscious use of sports and physical challenges during school time can greatly reduce the level of aggression in students. Encourage your kids to go out and work it off if they are angry. If you can, get out and run with them around the neighborhood. The results are nothing less than amazing.

Dynamic Writing: When angry, one way to find calm and clarity about the situation is to write it out. Giving yourself permission to write, unedited and freely, is like screaming into your pillow, but instead you do it silently on paper. It can be extremely relieving.

When things have built up and you don't know what else to do, write down whatever is on your mind, not paying attention to grammar (no commas or periods, no capitals or correct spelling necessary—kids love that part) or to content. Unfinished sentences are just fine. There are no rules. The idea is to keep your pen and mind in motion, letting the paper take all of the frustration out of you and put it into black and white until you lose steam, or until two pages are full. Not only is this cathartic, but being able to "voice" what is really bothering you offers no less than amazing results. Insights not expected, and feelings repressed, come forth and can be released and even utilized. Try it out yourself the next time you feel fit to be tied!

Conflict Resolution

What you want your children to learn is not only how to resolve conflict peacefully, but why it is important to do so. Fighting it out verbally or with fists only leads to perpetuated conflict, hurt feelings, if not worse, and negativity for all involved. Even when implementing all of the tools for anger and impulse mastery, emotional mastery, and good communication skills, conflicts still come about. In this section, the text is presented as if you are the facilitator in the conflict resolution process, rather than as a participant in it. It is important you empower your children with these skills instead of handling it for them.

In solving conflict, it is important to keep certain key points in mind:

- Select an appropriate time and place to resolve the conflict.
- Gather all of the facts without judgment.
- Allow each person to share her viewpoint.
- Practice active listening—first to understand, then to seek resolution.
- Use I Messages when speaking.
- Involve all parties in brainstorming for solutions.
- Be willing to compromise.

Core Success Tools for You

Conflict Resolution

The Parameters of Problem Solving

The following are the steps and components of effective and fair problem solving:

1. Clarify and define the conflict (observe what happened—do not interpret)
2. Use engaged listening and I Messages
3. Share feelings—state your viewpoint
4. Brainstorm solutions
5. Seek a solution
6. Make appropriate apologies

Clarify and Define the Conflict

In order to solve a problem, it must first become clear what the problem is. If two or more people are involved in the conflict, then there will be at least two different versions of what has occurred. It is important to hear all sides in order to get the big picture. Only then can you move into resolution.

What happened, when, and how? Usually the stream of explanations and indignations come rushing. Hold on, take a moment, and decide to work on the issue and not on the person you are angry with. Stick to the facts, which means what your senses observe, without adding personal interpretation. Help the children understand that the problem exists BETWEEN people, not in people. Getting this idea is crucial to the clarification process. If a child grasps that someone she is angry at isn't bad, but simply did something the child did not want or was hurtful, has a very different viewpoint, or perhaps even has similar feelings to his own, then children can begin to work it out together. So, the first thing necessary is to address the problem. Explain as clearly and concisely as possible what happened, without blaming, calling names, or belittling. Address the broken item or the injury. I messages are key here. You (parent/adult) as the neutral party should reflect back to the speaker, whoever it is, to be sure you got his part of the story straight. A template of this process, which can be used in almost any situation, can be downloaded at https://coresuccess.com/services/business-development/.

Using Engaged Listening and I Messages

Often we are amazed how small children can reiterate, verbatim, snatches of conversation, words, and other trivia that we didn't even know they'd heard. The reason they can do that so well is that beginning in infancy little ones are always busy taking in information. Everything is new and with their senses they soak up everything around them, putting the pieces of their world together. This is one reason that it is paramount to watch your language, especially around children. As they grow older, having "heard" the same messages so often, they stop hearing new things being said and instead, believing to already "know" what is being said, do not really take note of the meaning the sender this time intends. This is where their listening stops. They believe to hear that which they already know, what they expect to hear, or have already heard. Indeed they will often argue that they know *exactly* what was said and are surprised to find out that, more often than not, they were quite off base.

Core Success Tools for You

Engaged Listening

The key to engaged listening sounds simple, because it is. But practicing it can be challenging: The essential element necessary for good listening is turning off your own inner dialogue while another person is talking. It is important to not prepare a response while someone is speaking. Choose rather to clear your mind of its chatter. Set the intention to "want to know." Be sincerely interested in what the other person is going to say, and then hear it for the first time, sincerely hear it. This is not the same old story. Allow her input to arrive in your mind and take the time to understand. Then, and only then, decide upon your own response to what was shared. You don't need a long time for that, milliseconds actually, and then share easily.

Engaged listening at this level, with no mind static and with sincere interest, engages one easily into amazing interaction and connection with other people. You will sense a very different quality to your conversations, even in the conflicts that arise. They lose their frantic, competitive quality. Active listening opens doors for the other person, the speaker, as well. To be heard, to be truly listened to and heard on a deep level, is a gift of connection most of us long for.

Sharing Feelings—Stating Your Viewpoint

With the intention and tools in place for active and engaged listening, allow each person to give his experience of and feelings about the situation and note the facts as they emerge from the stories using the listening skills discussed. Monitor and encourage the use of I messages and all that entails. Also encourage active listening and all of its components. And remember that no one is right. Each person perceived what he or she did, what the other person did, and has a right to feel as she does. Feelings and viewpoint are not to be contested or discussed. They are neither wrong nor right, just different takes on the same issue. Allow those different versions to stand side-by-side, free of judgment. However, the facts, as best as possible, do need to be nailed down and, if possible, agreed upon by both parties.

For example, two girls were fighting. Someone accused the other of stealing and verbal and physical fighting ensued. During the resolution process, each of them obviously had her version of what happened. Liv accused Shelly of stealing her CD. Shelly accused Liv of breaking into her locker. Both of the girls have their story of what happened. During the sharing, done with active listening and nonjudgment, this is the story broken down: Liv said that her CD went missing 2 days ago (Fact). It had been in her locker (Fact). Before it went missing, Shelly had been asking to borrow it (Fact). Liv felt Shelly wasn't careful with her things and didn't want to lend the CD to Shelly (Viewpoint and Opinion). Liv saw Shelly walking down the hall with the CD in her hand (Fact). Shelly said that Liv had put the CD into Shelly's locker (Viewpoint). Shelly decided to listen to the CD (Fact). Liv saw Shelly with CD (Fact). She knew Shelly had stolen it out of her locker (Viewpoint).

The interesting thing about this story is that there were facts and viewpoints mixed together. And, guess what? THAT IS CONFLICT! That's what makes conflict resolution both a challenge and, at the very same time, also a very logical and effective solution-oriented process. Yes, we like that.

So, what actually happened with Shelly and Liv? Well, as the facts emerged and questions were asked, the following scenario came to light. Shelly and Liv have their lockers right next to each other. Jim, who's good friends with both girls, found the CD on the ground in front of Liv's locker and knew it was hers. He decided to just pop it back into her locker and, so, slipped it into the slots at the top. However, he had slipped it into Shelly's locker by mistake and not Liv's. That's how Shelly got the CD, not by stealing it! Although not all conflicts are clear cut, they all do have the viewpoint/fact mixture going on in each person's story. That's how we humans are. So, separating fact from viewpoint is paramount to the resolution process.

Brainstorm Solutions

Moving on to the solution-seeking part of conflict resolution brings us to brainstorming. This is a basic tool in many aspects of problem solving. Brainstorming helps all parties become involved in the solution-seeking process. It allows for the widest variety of possible solutions and, in itself, supports the reconciliation of parties in conflict. Follow the simple rules for brainstorming, explaining specifically to the children how this step will be done.

Brainstorming basics:

- Any and all ideas are welcome, even the crazy, seemingly impossible ones.
- Put as many ideas out onto the table as possible.
- Do not interrupt, discuss, or judge any suggestions until all possibilities are exhausted.

Seeking a Solution

After brainstorming has taken place, review each suggestion and sort out. Retain those ideas that are safe, fair, and doable and omit the rest. Discuss these options with the group. Then let the group decide on one solution that should be tried first to solve the conflict. Break that solution down into practical steps, naming the persons who are to take which steps. Assist the children in figuring out how to then implement the steps of the solution.

Appropriate Apologies

In making amends or compromising on an issue, children can be reminded that they don't lose anything by helping to rectify a situation. Just the opposite is true. By taking ownership of their part, they will feel good about it, create good will, and maybe even gain the respect of others. If a verbal apology is too difficult, encourage the child to put the apology into writing. The intention of an apology is to take responsibility, not to admit "wrongness" as a person.

Core Success Tools for You

Appropriate Apologies

When an apology is called for, young people can be assisted in the process by following these short steps:

Use the person's name:	*Tyler*
Say you are sorry:	*I apologize*
State what for:	*for spreading that rumor about you.*
Making it good again:	*I'llsetitrightbytellingthetruthof the matter; I won't do it again.*

Facilitating Conflict Resolution

When working out conflict situations, knowing the traditional mediation outline is very useful. You can use the steps outlined here as a guide. If you practice even some of these steps on a regular basis, you will find a culture of conflict resolution developing in your home, no matter the age of the kids that is very different and quite pleasant.

In our home, as we began integrating these tools with our kids, it became obvious that kids visiting our home were used to a very different way of dealing with things. At first, I was very involved in helping the kids work out issues, large or small, teaching them to listen and use I Messages, either using this outline or using the talking stick (as in the activity Talking Stick Untangler). As time went on, though, our kids began grabbing the talking stick without asking me for help. Then, I began to hear them with their friends or even sibling on the trampoline, sitting at the computer, under the fort of blankets, asking questions of the other person, and then saying: "so, if I understand you correctly, you feel that ..." And then they would solve the issue together and calmly. It was a trip to watch. Kids will emulate just about anything. Why not practice behavior that is so hugely helpful for them to emulate?

•

Core Success Tools for You

Facilitating Conflict Resolution

Step 1: Introductions and Rules

- Explain that the parties must want to resolve the problem.
- Everyone will get to talk and there's no interrupting, arguing, or fighting.
- Decide who will go first (can flip a coin).

If they don't agree to these rules, let them cool down first and then try again later.

Step 2: What Happened?

- Remind the kids to use I Messages when speaking and active listening when not. Each party will have a chance to give their story. One person speaks at a time, at length, until finished.
- Ask open-ended questions that cannot be answered with a "yes" or "no." Some examples of open-ended questions / nondirective questions are:
  - What happened?
  - What did you do?
  - How do you feel?
  - When did this start?
  - What bothers you most?
- You as the adult reflect back to the speaker what you've heard, for accuracy, and ask if there's anything else she wants to say.

Step 3: Brainstorming for Solutions

- Explain the following rules of brainstorming a possible solution:
  - All ideas should be shared, even seemingly crazy ones.
  - Avoid interrupting, discussing, or judging any suggestions.
  - Come up with as many ideas as possible.
- You can help the brainstorming process by asking the following questions:
  - What would you like to see happen?
  - What do you want?
  - What can you do to help resolve the problem?

Step 4: Reasonable Resolutions

- The mediator asks each disputant, independently, which ideas he likes best from the brainstormed list.
- Work with the kids until a resolution to the problem is agreed upon:
    - Will the result be a win-win solution?
    - Are both parties equally involved in the solution?
    - What are the exact details and steps of the solution?
    - Will the problem then be solved?
- If no resolution can be found, go back to the brainstorming process and find some more and different options.

Step 5: Coming to Closure

- Summarize what's been agreed upon.
- Acknowledge the disputants for having worked through their problem and for having found a solution peacefully.

Facilitating resolution and practicing these steps, you'll become quite skilled at using the tools necessary for conflict resolution. This skillfulness will have a profound effect on other areas of your life. Studies show that children who have worked as peer mediators at school are more likely later to take on roles of leadership in the community and in their jobs later in life. Your children will learn the structure of solving conflicts in this manner and will take these skills as well into their daily experiences with others. It is a long-term and intensely useful process for all involved to master.

Just remember: Not all conflicts can be mediated. Many require adult intervention and using the event to teach problem-solving skills.

Conclusion

You, as a parent, are a role model whether you want to be or not. You can take that fact and use it to offer your children positive examples for dealing with the challenges everyone faces. It is you who must first model these skills in order for your children to resolve conflict and deal with one another humanely. Teaching the skills is the next step of the learning process. Use teachable moments, those moments throughout the day that lend themselves to teaching these very skills, to empowering your child.

There is no perfect world and no quick fixes. Wherever people are living and working together there will be conflict. Practicing the ideas and skills offered here will help transform the atmosphere and the behavior of your children and your home. Your kids will have concrete steps they can use when confronted with situations that can feel overwhelming and frightening in other circumstances. The use of these skills will give them a sense of power and well-being and will groom them in the art of peaceable relations and fulfilling interactions.

CORE Success Factors of Resolving Conflict

CLARITY	OWNERSHIP	RESOLUTION	EXCELLENCE
Know and express feelings Define conflict Know resolution steps	Differentiate external vs. internal focus Ban blame Take responsibility	Defuse sibling rivalry Use active listening Practice I vs. You Messages Manage anger and impulsiveness Use the steps to resolve conflict Brainstorm solutions	Develop emotional maturity Practice empathy Know your triggers Calm and center self Share feelings

Keys to CORE Success

⚷ Conflict can be resolved.

⚷ Seek to understand. Be curious.

⚷ Trust that each person has a reason for their behavior.

⚷ Don't judge, use assessment.

⚷ Focus on facts.

⚷ Love the person, solve the problem.

⚷ Use the tools.

⚷ Stay calm or take a time out yourself.

Challenges and FAQs

√ *Just understanding hasn't done the trick. It seems my kids are exploiting my desire to understand them and not much is changing.* The patterns that have been in place in the family dynamics will take some time to change. It is vital that the rules are made cooperatively and are adhered to firmly. Understanding your child's reason for misbehavior does not mean there will be no consequences. The intention is for the child to learn discipline and respectful behavior. Although behavior can change through discussion, understanding, and resulting insight, most often change takes place and learning occurs when one experiences the consequences of one's behavior. Be clear, be loving, be firm, and be consistent.

√ *It seems I keep defaulting to punishment when I think I'm giving consequences. What's the difference again?* Most important to keep in mind is that the intention is for the child to learn something that will lead to new, responsible, and healthy behavior. If, for example, your child does not clean up the kitchen after dinner, although it is his task to do so, having him miss dinner is (1) not directly related to the event and (2) will not teach him about contributing and responsibility.

In this example, have the child cook the next meal from start to finish: cook, set the table, serve, and clean up afterward so he will gain experience in the amount of work involved to create meal. The odds of him then cleaning up the kitchen when it is again his turn to do so will be much higher since now he has the personal experience, and most likely the understanding, of the workload involved in cooking a meal and the need to share the responsibilities in the kitchen.

√ *We've created the rules together and my teenager consistently does not stick to the rules, even with consequences. I'm frustrated!* As kids start growing into their independence, they often feel they no longer have to adhere to rules and regulations that apply to younger children, or simply those that don't suit their desires. Unfortunately, this is normal teen behavior that, nonetheless, needs to be addressed directly and firmly.

Get clear, first with yourself and/or with your partner,

about what your limits are. How much are you willing to tolerate? What are your most "severe" consequences? Where are your boundaries? When that is clear, share it straight up with your child. Let them know where you stand and what action you will take. And then, take it! This is *the* vital step, so be super clear before you have that chat where you stand and what you are seriously willing to carry out.

When my son turned 18 he decided that the Internet curfew of 10 P.M. on school nights no longer applied to him, consistently flipping back on the modem to surf the net until all hours. The result was a surly child, tardiness, and slacking in schoolwork and chores due to being tired. Since his disregard for common house rules had been an ongoing issue, and he suddenly had zero agreement of house rules he didn't like, I got clear that if he no longer adhered to the house rules that served everyone, including my other child, then it was clear that he could no longer live in the house. Changing the rules we had all agreed upon and that served the common good was not an option.

It was certainly not my desire for him to move out, but the alternative was untenable for me and for my daughter. Faced with the choice, and knowing I was fully committed to carrying out the consequences, my son did choose to remain at home and to adhere to the rules we'd set together. To assist him and our well-being, I went over the rules with him and tweaked a few to more appropriately address his age and need for, and right to, more independence.

ANCHOR WITH ACTIVITIES

Dealing with Anger

What's the point?

To help children identify how they feel and what happens to their body when they are angry. To help children develop skills to deal with anger in an appropriate way.

What do I need?

Chart paper, markers, CORE Success Notebook, and from Appendix: worksheets When I'm Angry and Role-plays: Dealing with Feelings.

What do I do?

Discuss with children the following:

- How do you feel when you are angry?
- What changes begin to happen in your body when you are angry?

Examples: They may have answers like: *My heart beats faster, I get red in the face, I get tense, I feel like I'm ready to explode.*
Ask the children and discuss:

- Do you think that it's a good idea to handle a conflict when you feel like this? Why or why not?
- What might happen?
- What should we do?

Give the kids the worksheet "When I'm Angry" and then chat about it. Children can write down their thoughts in their CORE Success Notebooks.
Next, pair up family members. Give each pair a role-play. Have each pair do the role-play showing that they are very angry and have not

calmed down before dealing with the conflict. Then have them do the same role-play showing how they calm down first before dealing with the conflict. The conflicts don't have to be resolved in this role-play. The purpose here is to show the importance of calming down before dealing with conflict and not to react impulsively to feelings of anger.

Take it a step further

- What was the reaction of the person who received the other person's anger?
- Was that an appropriate way of dealing with anger? Why or why not?
- What happened when the person calmed down first before dealing with the conflict?
- Which method worked best? Why?

Listen and Share Mats

What's the point?

To help children to understand what they, themselves, are feeling and to learn to articulate that feeling. To help children develop empathy by listening to where another person stands and how they feel. To help diffuse a conflict situation and gain clarity in confusion.

What do I need?

Two large floor mats of a sturdy material, each a different color (door mats or heavy colored construction paper can be used if necessary). Each mat is divided by lines into four sections. One mat will be used as the Listening Mat and one as the Speaking Mat. The four sections on each mat should mirror one another in their location and be labeled as follows: Thoughts, Feelings, Wants, Action.

THOUGHTS	FEELINGS
WANTS	ACTION

What do I do?

Explain to the children that when you have a disagreement with someone, you can spend your time trying to convince them about your viewpoint, or that you are right and they are wrong. The other option is to spend your time more effectively and more pleasantly (!) by sharing your experience, in a way that can best be heard, and by listening to what another person perceives or feels. This enables you to understand one another and then find solutions together by asking for what you would like. This is how it goes:

1. Place the two mats on the floor a short distance away from one another. Declare one mat the Listening Mat and the other the Sharing Mat.

2. Then ask for two volunteers and have one person stand on each mat. The person on the Sharing Mat starts in one quadrant, such as, the feeling quadrant. The person on the listening mat goes to the respective quadrant on her mat, in this case the feeling quadrant. The person on the Sharing Mat tells the listener what is going on for him in that particular area, such as what feelings he has at the moment, while the person on the Listening Mat listens from their feeling quadrant.

For example, while standing on the Sharing Mat feeling quadrant the speaker might say, "I feel really angry when I share my music with you, but

I don't get any from you." And on the Thoughts section, might say, "I think we could both share or it's not fair." On the Wants section perhaps might say, "I'd like to have a copy of your Nickleback CD."

3. The speaker does not visit the Action quadrant yet. That will be visited when both persons have been speaker and listener and all wants have been shared.

4. The speaker and listener then change places (mats) and roles. Repeat the three segments in this new constellation.

5. When both parties have listened and shared quadrants 1–3, they may move to the Action section and then enter into negotiation as to what actions will take place. As they each stand on the Action square, they can ask the other person for a specific action that would be helpful or pleasant for them. They stay here until a resolution is reached.

Note: It is best to let the speaker continue through the three quadrants and see if questions are answered before they are posed by the listener. However, if questions are posed, they should be only in reference to the quadrant that is being addressed at that time. Questions may be asked if something is completely unclear or information is missing. Be sure not to let Listener begin speaking after he has posed a question.

Modeled after an exercise by Roy Anderson.

Talking Stick Untangler

What's the point?

To help children resolve conflicts that have become heated or are at a dead end. To train the usage of active listening and of I-messages.

What do I need?

A stick, decorated, whittled or painted—preferably by the kids. Another object such as a ball, crystal, or rock can also be used.

What do I do?

Explain to the children that over the centuries many native cultures have used a conflict resolution ritual using a talking stick to allow a fair and thoughtful flow to a conversation. They also use this ritual when parties are no longer able to calmly resolve an issue or when a seemingly dead end has been reached.

There will be only <u>one Sender and one or more Receivers</u> at any given time. Explain that all parties will be given the same opportunity to share their view of the situation, so it really does not matter who goes first. The children, or if necessary an adult, will decide who will play the role of the Sender first. All parties sit in a circle. Keeping eye contact is very constructive. The adult can help the children follow these simple rules.

The Sender's (speaker's) task is to share his perception of the situation using I-messages as much as possible; refrain from blame, cross words, insults, or belittling others; and concentrate on expressing his own feelings, motivation, and experience in/of the situation.

The Receiver's (listener's) task is to listen quietly, preferably without preparing a response; to not interrupt, make faces, or sounds of any kind indicating rejection, disagreement, or distraction.

The Talking Stick Round

1. The first Sender shares her experience.
2. After the first person talks, the stick is passed on to the next speaker and that person then has the floor. This is repeated until all parties have shared their perception of the situation.
3. Then, the adult can ask the parties to summarize what they have heard the other people say. This step also practices empathy. This helps people understand that there are many ways to view and feel in a particular situation. Use the talking stick also here to indicate your turn to give the summary.
4. Then a solution round is made with the stick. This time each person has the chance to offer a solution to the situation considering what's been heard of each party's position and needs.

5. In a general discussion, with or without the stick, a solution is agreed upon. This step will most likely come from the children themselves. If needed, however, the adult can help suggest a win-win solution to be followed through with.
6. Peace-making. Acknowledge the children for working through the process and finding a solution to their problem. Ask them to acknowledge their own input and willingness as well. Before breaking the circle, have the parties shake hands, or hug, as the case may be.

Note: Whenever a general discussion seems chaotic or starts to become contentious, reinstate the talking stick and its rules again.

CHAPTER 7

Abolishing Bullying

School Days ... Cruel Days ...

... A 15-year-old Irish girl was bullied at her new Massachusetts high school. After receiving threatening text messages and being tormented on Facebook, Formspring, and Twitter, she hanged herself in a stairwell at home.

... The beating started when the student was 5 years old and the bullying by the same person continued for 15 years.

... An 11-year-old boy just wanted to fit in but was often left in tears and despair by the taunts, laughter, and physical abuse of schoolyard children who bullied.

.... A 14-year-old Vancouver student hanged herself shortly after speaking on the phone with girls who bullied her. One 16-year-old girl was found guilty of criminal harassment and uttering threats; another was acquitted.

... After a long period of bullying at school, and just 6 days after his 13th birthday, Jared B. High took his own life at home.

... Two heavily armed teenagers went on a bloody rampage at

Columbine High School in Littleton, Colorado, killing 12 students and 1 teacher before committing suicide. Students have said the gunmen were bullied and excluded at school.

... Fifteen-year-old Greg Doucette was so tormented about his acne by bullies at Notre Dame Secondary School that he hanged himself in the basement of his home.

... Chino Hills, California, June 2015, from a 16-year-old boy's suicide note: "One of the biggest reasons why I killed myself is to prevent suicides. I want to prevent anyone I can from hurting." The teen took his life with the belief his death would make bullies think twice about their actions.

The Core Point ... and Your Gain

Bullying has, sadly, not only become commonplace in the lives of our youth, but it has taken on drastic proportions of violence, cruelty, public humiliation, and is ever more often resulting in fatal events. It most frequently goes unseen by outsiders and unreported by bystanders. It is seriously harmful and can be stopped. What's necessary is that you, as parents, enable your children to understand, expose, and help stop bullying. You can do this by empowering your children to advocate, for themselves and others.

With many reports of aggression, violence, shootings, and suicides in many areas of the world, it is obvious that bullying is a very serious problem and has devastating results. However, it is not a new problem and there have always been people who bully in every walk of life and at all ages. Bullying exists everywhere, but often remains hidden. It's important to remember that these tragic cases are the ones that hit the news. Widespread bullying goes on every day unreported, yet the damage is still extreme.

What Bullying Is

There is a difference between bullying and conflict. Conflict is a disagreement that happens when people want different things or do not agree on something. The people involved have more or less equal power, and there is not an intention at the outset to hurt someone. Usually, in conflict the parties involved are motivated to find a solution to the problem.

You, as a parent, need to empower your children to understand, expose, and to help stop bulling.

You, as a parent, need to empower your children to understand, expose, and to help stop bulling.

Bullying can be described as intimidating or threatening behavior toward a weaker person or someone at a disadvantage in some way. It can be easily identified as being one-sided, unfair, and often repeated. An uneven distribution of power always exists between the person bullying and the victim (this is what clearly distinguishes it from conflict). Bullying behaviors include physically hurting or threatening to hurt someone, repetitive insults and name-calling, derogatory gossip and rumors, social exclusion, and sexual bullying that can be anything from innuendos to improper touching. Those who bully thrive on the sense of power and control they get from their bullying behaviors.

According to the Bureau of Justice Statistics (2006), bullying happens most commonly to middle school youth, with almost 50 percent of them reporting having been bullied. Fifteen to 25 percent of students overall are frequently bullied, and 15 to 20 percent of students bully others often. Of students surveyed, around 20 percent have been bullied physically while almost a third experienced bullying of some kind (Luxenberg et al., 2014).

Statistics from our newest form of bullying - cyber bullying that uses the Internet, social media sites, and texting to intimidate and antagonize - showed in 2003 that 35 percent of kids were threatened online. Twenty-one percent received mean or threatening emails or other messages, and 58 percent did not tell their parents, or any adult, about something mean or hurtful that happened to them online.

Years ago bullying was not recognized or dealt with. Victims of bullying had two options: to handle the problem quietly by trying to avoid it, or to resort to violence to stop it. Neither solves the problem and neither stops the bullying behaviors in the long term. Back then, people did not realize the seriousness of bullying and the long-term psychological and emotional impact on the victims. Most people who bully were once victims themselves, so the cycle continues. (See Appendix, Is this Bullying? Take the quiz with your kids.)

Unfortunately, parents often practice behaviors toward their own children that can be categorized as bullying. You are in a power position with your children, your behavior is often repeated. If it is unfair or emotionally or physically harming, it is bullying. Although this is not an easy thing to admit, it is vitally important to take ownership of any and all behaviors that you may have that fall into this category. Our children learn their behavior—it is not innate. Children who are bullied, or who bully, have learned their behavior either at home, at school, in the extended family, or in social settings.

If your behavior could be viewed as bullying in any way, change it. Here are the tools to do so. If not, use these tools to help your kids deal with any bullying they may encounter in their lives. It's your job as a parent to be sure that your home is a safe, healthy, supportive, and loving environment where positive behavior is trained and solid self-esteem is developed. By providing the positive connections at home, you provide the best assurance to abolish bullying from the lives of your children.

This chapters covers all sides of bullying, and the most important things for your children to know include:

- What exactly bullying is
- What their options are for dealing with it
- When it is safe to take a stand and when they should get help
- What the difference is between tattling and reporting
- What they can do to be part of the solution

The Impact of Bullying

In a landmark study, started in Great Britain in 1958, the National Development Study of more than 180,000 people from birth through today, 10,000 of whom were still in the study 50 years later, "researchers found that people who were bullied either occasionally or frequently continued to suffer higher levels of psychological distress decades after the bullying occurred. They were more likely than study subjects who were never bullied to be depressed, to assess their general health as poor, and to have worse cognitive functioning. In addition, those who were bullied frequently had a greater risk of anxiety disorders and suicide" (Kaplan, 2014).

The impact of bullying is widespread, having a very detrimental effect educationally, physically, and psychologically.

The educational impact includes:

- Finding it hard to pay attention
- Not wanting to talk much in school
- Lower academic performance
- Not wanting to go to school, or thinking about changing school
- Missing school due to being physically sick from the stress, anxiety, and fear of being bullied

The emotional and psychological impact on a child include:

- Embarrassment
- Low self-esteem
- Feeling unsafe
- Fearful of becoming less popular, not fitting in, and of being a social failure
- Anxiety
- Fear

Being bullied can lead to further peer rejection and the development of a cycle in which the children who are most in need of support from their peers are the least likely to receive it.

"Our children need to be able to see us take a stand for a value and against injustices, be those values and injustices in the family room, the boardroom, the classroom, or on the city streets."

BARBARA COLOROSO

Core Success Tools for You

The Impact of Bullying

Take a moment of time from reading this and do a small exercise. After you read these instructions, take 5 minutes to follow them through.

Close your eyes for a moment. Get comfortable and just listen to your breathing and feel yourself relax onto the surface you're sitting on. Now let your mind wander back to your own childhood and think to a time when either you were bullied, or you remember someone else being bullied. Recall that scene. Who was involved? What exactly happened? How did you feel in that situation? What was your part in the bullying? How did the situation finally play out? What would you wish would have happened differently if you had the chance to re-do how the situation took place?

Open your eyes. Note for yourself how recalling that situation affects how you are feeling right now.

The Parties Involved

There are three parties involved in almost every bullying situation: those who bully, those who are bullied, and the bystanders, or observers. Some bullying situations do go unobserved, unfortunately, in which case you do not have a bystander. Each of these parties plays their part and you must educate your children about the different parties as well as what each can do to end bullying.

Children Who Bully

Children who bully others tend to have certain traits, mainly because causing, or wanting to cause, harm to others stems from an inner personal dissatisfaction turned outward in an unhealthy way. Here are some traits that are common to children who bully others:

- Have been bullied themselves
- Have low self- esteem
- Feel the need to dominate others
- Show little empathy toward others

- Are often impulsive
- Have inadequate problem-solving skills
- Have inappropriate social skills
- Are unable to deal with their emotions adequately
- Use aggression to deal with emotions, especially anger
- Use aggression as an outlet for their problems
- Are seeking attention
- Get a sense of control and power from bullying
- Enjoy this power and control and abuse it

Children Who Are Bullied

There is no rule that determines which children get bullied and which do not. However, there are some factors that have come to light with time that are useful to know. Children who are bullied have been known to have one, or some, of the following traits:

Active Traits	Passive Traits
Problems concentrating	Avoid confrontation
Act irritated	Do not seek peers for help
Make fun of others	Have difficulties finding friends
Practice socially irritating behavior	Emotionally busy creating safety
Have ADD, or similar	Males show lack of sensitivity
Are remedial learners	Close relationship with their parents
Have special needs	

Please know that it is not always the case that kids who are bullied have these traits or that kids without these traits don't get bullied. They are mentioned here for you to be aware of as you build your knowledge base of bullying.

Bystanders

In most situations of bullying, but of course not all, there are other people who witness the bullying. This can be friends of the person bullied, friends of the person doing the bullying, or simply bystanders who have no affiliation but are aware it is happening. This party in the bullying issue is a very important one. Anyone who knows that bullying is happening or who witnesses a bullying situation as a bystander has a responsibility to act.

It's our job to make children aware of the importance of their role as bystanders, the impact of "Bystander Power" and "Kid Power." If they know that bullying is happening, they must realize that it is their responsibility to do something to help solve the problem. Kids have to know they have the power to change the situation. As bystanders, a group of children have a significant influence on the outcome of bullying. They are more likely to witness bullying more frequently than adults. Also, children tend to look to other children for cues on how to respond to bullying situations. Viewing bullying is often distressing for children. They may feel confused and they don't know what to do, or if they do know what to do, they are afraid to act in defense of the person being bullied. Consequently, many children may just ignore the bullying and walk away. Or they may provide an audience by standing around and watching. They often provoke the situation by encouraging the person who is bullying or even joining in themselves.

Adults and Bullying

Adults can have a very positive impact on the problem of bullying. As parents and teachers, you must realize your responsibility for providing a safe environment for your children at all cost. Your children must feel that they can turn to you and that they can trust you to help them and keep them safe.

Intervention by adults has an extraordinary impact on children who feel bullied. Children feel reassured and empowered when adult intervention takes place. It shows that you do not condone any of this behavior and that you care. However, the unfortunate reality is that most children suffer in silence and do not report their experiences to adults. Why is this? Reasons include:

- Belief that no one will do anything
- Belief that adults will not intervene effectively
- Belief that nothing will change
- An unwillingness to publicize their own unpopularity
- Feeling too confused, upset, or afraid
- Fear of taunts or accusations of tattling

- Fear of revenge/retaliation from the person who bullied them

Adults play a vital role and must be actively and consistently involved. Only then will the solution to bullying begin. If your children know they can tell you anything, you are halfway home to resolving any bullying issue that they encounter.

Advocating, Refusing, Reporting, and Tattling

Standing up for yourself, or for another, is a powerful step to take. Children can be helped to do this by learning to advocate in a bullying situation or to report if the situation feels unsafe or they feel unable. Standing up on one's own is not advisable unless one has back-up and feels totally safe in doing so. Advocating for someone who is being bullied is actually the most effective way to abolish bullying situations. (See Appendix, Is it Safe?)

Advocating for a person being bullied means you can take a stand, or get help. If you are a bystander and see bullying taking place, speaking up, asking a question, or even coming to the aid of the person being bullied can put an abrupt end to a bullying event. This may not always be safe or smart to do. In order to differentiate whether it is or not, it would be useful, as stated later in this chapter, for the school to conduct a bullying awareness program at the school. That way all children and adults are informed. However, if your child is a bystander, encourage him in any case to go and get help. Never assume it will work out or the child being bullied can "take care of himself." One does not know that. Bullying often turns harsh and people can get seriously injured. (See Appendix worksheet Should I Refuse or Report?)

Refusing is an empowered way to turn bullying around. There are skills a child can learn to face bullying straight on and stop it. They cannot do that alone. They need support from an adult and training in self-assertion and to build their self-esteem (see Chapter 4, *Raising Self-Esteem*). If your child feels like the situation is safe and would like to stop the bullying on her own, give your child some tools and tips to do so. (See Appendix, Refusing Bullying with Confidence.)

Reporting is taking action and informing a responsible adult with the desire to resolve the issue. The goal is to keep yourself and others safe, and telling an adult will make sure this happens. When children report it is extremely important that they are acknowledged for their courage to do so. It is also vital that they know you, as the adult, will do something about the bullying and you will not stop until the bullying stops. Encourage kids to report, and *report again*, if the bullying does not stop.

Tattling is seeking attention or having the desire to get someone into trouble. The main goal here is not about taking care of the person being hurt, but there is another agenda going on with the person tattling or they are getting something out of the event. Tattling should be called for what it is and not be rewarded. (See Appendix, Tattling vs. Reporting.)

Core Success Tools for You

Advocating, Refusing, Reporting, and Tattling

You want to teach your children to be able to recognize bullying and what to do when they encounter it. Here are some questions you can learn together, as well as suggestions on what steps to take.

Ask yourself these questions:

- Is the behavior harmful and/or threatening?
- Is it one-sided—meaning, one person has more power?
- Is it unfair?
- Has it happened before?
- Do you feel unsafe?

Take Action! If you find yourself in a bullying situation, or observing one, you can do the following:

- Ask yourself if you feel safe to refuse. (See Appendix, Is it Safe?) If so, use some one of the dealing with bullying strategies. (See Appendix, Refusing Bullying with Confidence.)
- If it is unsafe to refuse or advocate, get help. (See Appendix, How to Report Bullying.)

Strategies to Prevent Bullying

Children must be trained by adults, at home and in school, how to recognize and deal with bullying. They must understand that reporting bullying to an adult is a very effective tool in stopping bullying, and that it is completely different than tattling just to get someone in trouble.

Parents and teachers must help children develop empathy for others who are bullied, help them to realize they have a role in being a part of the solution, and teach them ways to eradicate the bullying. Adults who model the courage and skills to intervene, in turn, teach children the skill to model these qualities.

What strategies and skills can you teach your children to help them deal with bullying? The strength of friends, recognizing and advocating in bullying situations, and how to prevent it are key.

Friendship plays an important role in preventing bullying and in helping our children cope once it has occurred. Children who have a friend(s) are less likely to be bullied. If bullied, a child's friend(s) can help him deal with bullying by listening and giving advice and reporting the situation to an adult. Positive friendships are important in the overall social development of children. It is important that children know how to deal with friends who do not show mutual respect and caring or who pressure them into bullying others. (See Chapter 3, *Living to Thrive,* for activities on developing friendship skills.)

It is also essential that children who engage in bullying behaviors themselves to admit that they do in fact bully. You have to teach them how to recognize the problem and how to change their behavior. You must take this negative power away from children who bully and help them develop self-esteem and a positive self-image that will, in turn, empower them. Remember, the reasons a person bullies are due to low self-esteem and the need to feel control. Therefore, it is important that you take the initiative to help not just the person who is bullied, but also the person doing the bullying.

Core Success Tools for You

Strategies to Prevent Bullying

Here's what your kids need to know:

Recognize the Bullying.

Ask yourself...

- Is it harmful and threatening behavior?
- Is it one-sided?
- Is it unfair?
- Do you feel unsafe?

Refuse the Bullying.

- Decide whether it is safe to refuse on your own.
- Stay calm.
- Decide what strategies to use.
- If it is unsafe to refuse on your own, or it doesn't work, report the bullying and get help from an adult.

Use assertive skills only if you feel the situation is safe and feel confident.

- Stand up straight.
- Have good eye contact.
- Speak clearly and sound confident and calm.
- Respect the rights of others.
- Know and express your right to be treated fairly.

Prevent Bullying from happening to you.

- Stay close to friends.
- Make smart decisions.
- Stay in sight of peers and adults when possible.
- Don't be alone in places where you may be bullied.
- Don't set yourself up to be bullied.
- Don't provoke others or make situations worse.
- Don't brag about having money or expensive or about being better than others.

Develop your own self-confidence.

- Get involved in something that makes you feel good about yourself.
- Build solid friendships/join a team (see Chapter 3, Living to Thrive).
- Advocate for others when you see bullying happening, or get help by reporting it.

"If you are not part of the solution, you are part of the problem." Education in this area is crucial to teachers, other school staff, parents, and students. If your child is being bullied or you have reason to believe that she is bullying others, it is imperative to work together closely with the teachers and staff of the school. This book and training can be used to help the staff support your child, and all the children, to put a stop to bullying. As a parent, however, you can do a lot to help your children by increasing their awareness of bullying, identifying bullying behavior, and learning strategies of dealing with it.

The way you teach your children to respond to bullying has a definite effect on the outcome. Children must learn problem-solving strategies; how to be assertive and stand up for themselves; when it is safe to handle bullying on their own; when they must report; and when to seek intervention from an adult. Young people are our greatest resource for addressing violence and stopping bullying.

Bullying is Nothing New

The harmful emotional and psychological consequences of being bullied have been found to extend into adulthood in the form of lower self-esteem and increased risk for depression and mental health problems. The issue of bullying can be found in all walks, in all areas, of life and at all ages. Even in sports that train sportsmanship and team work, bullying is often found. In an interview concerning an NFL commissioned report on accusations of bullying on the Miami Dolphins, Jeff Fisher, coach of the St. Louis Rams, said about taunting during games: "We agreed we have an issue on the field, and we ... are going to get it under control as soon as we possibly can" (Belson, 2014).

Bullying is an issue that extends from youth onward, and one serious outcome of being bullied is that, in many cases, the person who is a victim of bullying becomes the one who bullies, especially in later life. So, the cycle of aggressive behavior continues into adulthood in the form of:

- Associating with others who have aggressive behavioral problems. An example is joining a gang.
- Verbally and physically abusing their spouse and/or children at home.

- Using bullying, sexual harassment, and social exclusion in the workplace.
- Bullying behaviors in social activities.
- Committing criminal acts.

Core Success Tools for You

Ending Bullying

What parents can do:

- Watch for signs in your child. Listen to what they share. Be available and build open communication.
- Build trust: Listen to, and believe, what your child tells you. Take your child seriously.
- Talk to the teachers and ask questions. You are not a bother; you are your child's advocate.
- Do not stop talking until you are satisfied things are going well.
- Ask for help for both parties—the person bullied and the person doing the bullying.
- Assure your child that he is not alone and that efforts to stop the bullying will work because you won't give up until it is better.

What children can do:

- Become good at identifying bullying.
- Learn how to deal with it or how to get help.
- Understand when to refuse, when to advocate, and when to report.
- Differentiate between tattling and reporting.
- Know that they are not alone.

Working with the Person Who Bullies

Working with children who are bullying is as crucial as helping children who have been bullied. Children who bully may do so for a variety of reasons.

Warning signs of a child who may bully in the future can start to show up early, even at the preschool age. Take the example of a little boy who seems to take pleasure in pushing a smaller boy off the swing or in forcibly taking his toys, often reducing the boy to tears. Younger children who bully can grow up to be youth who bully if an adult doesn't intervene and put a stop to the aggressive behavior. Children who bully may:

- Have been bullied themselves
- Have low self-esteem
- Need to dominate others
- Show little empathy toward others
- Often be impulsive
- Have inadequate problem-solving skills
- Have inappropriate social skills
- Be unable to deal with their emotions adequately
- Use aggression to deal with emotions, especially anger
- Use aggression as an outlet for their problems
- Be seeking attention
- Get a sense of control and power from bullying
- Enjoy this power and control and abuse it

You must help the children who bully to identify their behaviors, to develop a full understanding of the impact of their bullying, and to help them turn their behaviors around. You must teach them self-control and how to channel their negative emotions appropriately. You must help them develop a positive self-image and build their self-esteem and, thus, empower them to act in positive, caring ways toward themselves and others.

Long-term research studies have proven that many "problem" children, whose aggressive behavior goes unaddressed, fail in their ability to deal successfully with their lives and in the majority of cases become dependent on social support. They perform especially poorly in school and remain below their educational potential. In order to make up for their failure in performance and sense of being socially isolated, these children whose self-esteem has been severely damaged see escalated aggressive behavior as the only possibility to experience power and to prove themselves (UCLA Department of Psychology, n.d.).

To help a child who is bullying, it is vital to find out the source of the aggression and reason for the lack of self-esteem. In most cases, this is a longer process as the road to becoming someone who bullies is a long one. Finding professional help for the child is important. It is also necessary to include the family members in that process if the bullying behavior has a source in the family. Bullying will continue into future generations unless the cycle is stopped. Making sure that children who bully get help to turn things around will put an end to that cycle. Although bullying is devastating, the person who is bullying is in pain and in need of help. They will not be able to get themselves out of the situation alone.

Abolishing Bullying at School

In 2011 Westbrook Connecticut took a survey its middle and high school students, parents, and teachers. The results are similar to others around the country: 87 percent of faculty said that they do not witness verbal threats among students and 45 percent also don't see bullying often. Compare those rates to the 20 percent of students who reported receiving verbal threats pretty much daily (the national average of reported student bullying is 27 percent) and it becomes apparent that we have quite a problem: all too often the place where most bullying takes place, namely in school, is least awareness of the problem.

As a parent you can do something about that. First course of action is to contact the counseling center and the principal. Ask what bullying education is in place. If there is none, or you meet with resistance or dragging feet, turn to your school board. There are divisions attending to bullying, drug abuse, and alcohol use. Ask for an advocate to help initiate an antibullying program at your school. Be clear, fair, pleasant, and firm in your intention to enlist the school in the goal to abolish bullying from your child's school and life.

Core Success Tools for You

Abolishing Bullying

To effectively deal with bullying at school, you can take the following steps to help keep your child, and others, safe from bullying:

- Nurture and grow the trust and open communication between you and your children. If they know they can open up to you, they will tell you about situations of hurt and bullying in their life.
- Let your children know that they are not alone and that the adults around them will help them.
- Meet with your child's teachers to discuss details and persons involved in the bullying situation.
- Work to have the entire-school-approach implemented through a bullying awareness training. That is all staff, teachers, bus drivers, monitors, caretakers, volunteer personnel, etc. be involved in the training. A bullying prevention program for the students would be essential as well.
- Work with your school principal toward conducting a survey of staff, students, and parents to help determine the seriousness of the problem in the school, and if students and staff are aware of what it is, and what to do. It is helpful to conduct the survey both before and after students/staff/parents have had a bullying prevention program.
- Advocate for the school to establish and enforce antibullying policies. These would include:
    - Have parents involved in communication, education, and the implementation of a bullying prevention program.
    - The school is consistent and effective in action and follow-up to bullying situations with the victims, with the children who are bullying, and with the parents of both.
    - Provide necessary steps to ensure the safety of children who have been bullied when there is a chance of retaliation by the student who bullied.
    - The school provides necessary help for children who bully, such as anger management, ways to channel negative energy (e.g., sport programs), counseling, etc.
    - All students are encouraged to use their power as bystanders to help stop bullying. They should be acknowledged for doing so.
    - Increase supervision of children's behavior in lunchrooms, playgrounds, washrooms, on school buses—where bullying is most likely to occur.
    - Reinforcing the social skills and strategies taught as much as possible through real life situations so there is a transfer and application of what has been learned.

Conclusion

Bullying is tough, pervasive, and sometime scary. Together, however, bullying can be stopped. Information, education and empowerment is what can stop bullying. It is up to you. Everyone has the responsibility to help stop bullying because:

- It makes it difficult for those who bully others to succeed.
- It takes the audience and power away from the person who bullies.
- It gives support and help to the person who is being bullied.
- It helps to change ideas about bullying by giving the message that "bullying is not right and will not be tolerated."
- Doing something as a bystander demonstrates that it is everyone's responsibility to stop bullying.

You must be committed to giving the time, energy, and resources necessary to keep your children safe from bullying. The power for that is in your hands, not theirs, and they are worth it.

Using all of the elements of CORE Success is a powerful way to prevent bullying from even starting.

CORE Success Factors of Abolishing Bullying

CLARITY	OWNERSHIP	RESOLUTION	EXCELLENCE
Define what bullying is Know the impact of bullying Identify the parties involved	Advocate for those bullied Refuse bullying Report bullying	Prevention Be proactive Educate and advocate	Insist on zero tolerance for bullying Help the person bullied Help the person who bullies

Keys to CORE Success

⚷ Be alert! Bullying is the springboard for many violent acts. It is also the cause of most physical and emotional injury done at schools, being done on a consistent basis usually over a longer period of time. It must be taken seriously. If bullying is dealt with effectively, violent incidents at school will be greatly reduced.

⚲ Keep the channels of communication with your children wide open. Get to know their friends, be aware of mood shifts and comments that sounds fearful or self-harming.

⚲ If you are concerned about possible bullying activities, contact your school counselor, a trusted teacher, and your principal immediately.

⚲ Useful websites with resources and valuable links are:
  • Bully Online: bullyonline.org/
  • Stop Bullying: stopbullying.gov/
  • National Bullying Prevention Center: pacer.org/bullying/
  • Stomp Out Bullying: stompoutbullying.org/index.php/ ways-help/

Challenges and FAQs

√ *It seems very likely that my daughter is being bullied at school, but she refuses to talk with me about it.* Only she knows the reasons for her reticence to share, but don't give up being her advocate. Speak with her teachers and the counselor to get a clearer picture of behavior and any relationship or conflict issues going on. When you have some more information, create a safe space (time and location) to talk gently with your daughter.

Find out why she does not want to share with you, before you try to figure out what's happening for her. Ask engaged questions and trust that she wants your help. After that is clarified, and you have assured her that she can trust you implicitly to support her in a way that will be helpful and will also respect her wishes, invite her to share with you precisely what is going on. If it reaches a point of serious concern before she does share, though, tell her you are going to invite her to a meeting together with the counselor, or principal, whomever your daughter trusts more, to be sure that you and they, as her support team, do everything possible to open up and resolve the problem.

√ *I've spoken to the counselor and the principal, but they don't seem to be taking the bullying issue very seriously. I feel hopeless.* Statistics do prove that teachers and administration at a school drastically underestimate the frequency, and intensity, of bullying situations. If you find no support there, turn to the school board in your district. There will be a person responsible for school climate and/or parental emotional and social concerns. Inform your principal that you will be taking this step to get help, and then take it. If a school does not take reports of bullying seriously, there is a serious problem at the school level and must be addressed.

Note: By no means does this text cover all aspects of bullying, nor does it intend to equip you or your child with all the tools needed to face bullying that has gotten out of control. It will educate you on the basics of bullying and raise your awareness so you can enable your children to see potential bullying situations and hand you some tools to help your child deal with bullying from home. No book can adequately replace a bullying awareness and prevention program offered through a school your child is attending. Talk to the principal and advocate for a schoolwide program.

ANCHOR WITH ACTIVITIES

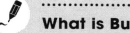

What is Bullying?

What's the point?

To develop awareness and understanding of what bullying is and how to recognize it.

What do I need?

Chart paper, pencils/crayons/markers, drawing paper, from Appendix: Bullying is... and Is this Bullying? sheets

What do I do?

Pass out drawing paper to each family member. Ask everyone to draw what they think a person who bullies looks like and then to write three to five characteristics of a person who bullies under the drawing. Talk about each person's drawing and the characteristics they named.

What should we talk about?

- Are these drawings very similar?
- Have you portrayed the person who bullies in the same way?
- How are the drawings different?
- Are the drawings just of boys? Of girls? Of young people? Of older people?

It's important that the children realize that people who bully are of all ages and gender, can look mean and intimidating, or can also look kind and friendly.

After discussing the above, write down "A Person Who Bullies" on the chart paper. Ask the children to share some of the characteristics of a person who bullies that they wrote below their drawing. Write down their responses.

Through the discussion, come up with an explanation of bullying. Write down what the family decides as a definition, then read it out loud. Compare it to the sheet "Bullying is..."

How do I continue the conversation?

- Is this description the same or similar to what you wrote? Discuss.
- What are the key words here? (Unfair, one-sided, and repeated)
- What is conflict? (Conflict is a disagreement that happens when people want different things. The people involved are not purposely trying to hurt each other and have equal power to try and solve the problem.)
- What is the difference between conflict and bullying? (An uneven distribution of power always exists between the person who bullies and the victim. In conflict, the distribution of power is more balanced.)
- How is bullying behavior unfair?
- How is bullying behavior one-sided?
- Is bullying serious? Why or why not?
- Is it everyone's problem? Why or why not?

Together with a child (one parent to one child if possible) work through the sheet "Is This Bullying?" Then discuss as a family.

What Can I Do?

What's the point?

To teach children how to respond to bullying. To teach children to recognize when it is safe to resist bullying on their own.

What do I need?

Chart paper, markers, from Appendix: What Can I Do?, Is It Safe?, and Should I Refuse or Report? sheets

What do I do?

On chart paper write "What Can I Do?" Ask your children what they can do if they are being bullied. Show the sheet, "What Can I Do?" and discuss it as a family.

Write on the chart paper "Is It Safe?" Ask children to give you examples of when it would be safe to stand up to the person who is bullying. Write down their answers. Review the sheet "Is It Safe." Discuss it with your children.

Note: Pass out the sheet "Should I Refuse or Report?" Work together, one parent and one child, if possible, and then discuss it with the entire family.

How do I continue the conversation?

Have children find examples of bullying in the newspaper, in movies, and on TV. Ask your children to write in their CORE Success Notebook how the characters in the show or article respond to the bullying and if their actions worked. Ask them then to write what the characters should have done if their actions were not useful or were inappropriate.

AFTERWORD

I
t is not possible to change your home and family life unless you are willing to be a student of yourself and to change how you operate. You, as a parent, are not only part of the system, but you actually comprise the system. Whatever your thoughts, your energies, what you do and teach, your daily activities—you are the architect and builder of your family. Unless you are willing to examine your own behavior, your way of seeing your children, your way of viewing the world, and yourself, the situation as it is will absolutely not change.

There is no doubt that society and the media have a large part to play in the negativity, violence, lack of responsibility, and lack of respect with which children today are confronted and in which they are being trained. Yes, there is a lot to counteract. Through consistent exposure to such behaviors, as taught in the media, kids learn these traits as a normal and acceptable way of behaving and interacting with one another and their world.

As parents, as educators, and caretakers, do take the time and energy to consciously decide what you are going to impart to these young people, how you want to role model behaviors that you wish for them to assimilate, and to seek ways to help them train positive behaviors.

You, alone, decide what your experience will be at any moment of the day, depending on how you choose to see events and people and how you choose to respond to them.

Building on the Positive

Looking at what is working and building on the positive offers a sense of enthusiasm for all involved. No doubt there are a myriad of areas that are working fantastically in your home. Acknowledge those events and the people creating them (especially yourself!) and use them as a springboard. Look at how those events or projects could be expanded upon, or even repeated, to give CORE Success a familiar and comfortable start in your home.

> *You, alone, decide what your experience will be at any moment of the day, depending on how you choose to see events and people and how you choose to respond to them.*

Each of you is the creator of the world as you see it. You, alone, decide what your experience will be at any moment of the day, depending on how you choose to see events and people and how you choose to respond to them. This awareness of being self-determined is a gift in creating a loving, happy, and responsible life for yourself, and then for your family as a result.

Big Picture Thinking

In order to maintain an enthusiastic and committed attitude, Big Picture Thinking is essential. Keeping a bird's eye view of what the mission is, who is responsible for what, and having the common good of all ever present in mind will greatly aid in all areas of working together.

Core Success Tools for You

Big Picture Thinking

Here's one way of working with this tool:

At the start of each family meeting ask those gathered what their personal commitment to this program is, as well as what their vision for your family is. Then ask them what their intention is for that very meeting—what they want to feel, contribute, and accomplish during that time. End the meeting by reading the family's mission statement. Allow what has been said to be felt in the room. Give that vision and intention space, and then build on it. Let it lift you up as you turn to the work at hand.

Brainstorming

To come up with ideas about how to approach a subject, a problem, or a dream, brainstorming is a boon! Brainstorming is a simple, yet highly effective tool to unleash the creative forces within individuals and especially in groups. It is a practical activity that can be used anytime that a new project is being started, a problem arises, a conflict seems to have no solution, or a vision is being born.

Brainstorming is a tool that you can use well in the family as you move down this road of CORE Success, whether it is in resolving a conflict, establishing a rule, or finding a solution to a problem the family, or a member, is facing. Brainstorming as a family hones skills, builds trust, and brings everyone into the process of growing into a more positive, easy, and happy family.

"You see things; and you say, 'Why?' But I dream things that never were; and I say, "Why not?"

GEORGE BERNARD SHAW

Core Success Tools for You

Brainstorming

All that is needed is for one person to be willing to take notes. Everyone is then asked to verbalize all ideas that they have concerning the given topic. No idea is too crazy, impractical, too expensive, or silly. Everything is thrown out into the room for perusal, without being judged or discussed. Write it all down as the ideas fly. After all those ideas have been bantered about, a selection process can take place. Each idea is then looked at for its usefulness, applicability, timeliness, etc. Read each aloud and let the group discuss its possibilities. Usually a few very good and effective ideas come out of this process. It can be as short as 5 minutes, or take an entire afternoon, depending on the size of the issue and the needs of the group (see activity in Chapter 2, Harnessing Hope).

During one training session, someone said that a home should be "perfectly harmonious." As wonderful as that sounds, and as much as we would all like to experience that, it is not a realistic possibility for our world. Looked at it a bit differently, that is the very neat thing! Home is a slice of this thing called life. It is not separate, nor should it be handled differently. With all of the joys, challenges, changes, and surprises that life as a family provides, your home and family are the perfect environment to develop CORE Success. You can use your relationships and daily experiences to strengthen your experience of success in all areas that have been presented here. You have the time and opportunity to practice guiding your children to discover and strengthen their sense of core success.

Love and fear are two motivating factors behind almost all of human behavior. And fear is the source of almost all of your negative thoughts, actions, and experiences. You may not ever be able to eliminate fear completely, but what you can do, and would be wise to strive toward, is to develop and nurture skills that help each person to recognize, deal, with and transform personal fears into personal power. That is something that is a byproduct of working with CORE Success. Each person can find the core of their own success. Fears that do arise in life can be looked at and worked with in a healthy and productive manner, rather than in an inhibiting and destructive manner. These are the concrete benefits and real rewards of committing to your own CORE Success. And, it all begins within each one of us individually, before it can ever be transported to "out there."

Each person is strengthened in who he or she is by choosing a positive perspective, raising self-esteem, learning conflict resolution, communicating effectively, and training tools for inner discipline and personal excellence. As a parent, you have the ability, and the responsibility, to revamp the lessons you teach your kids. CORE Success for Parents is one great path to set foot upon to help your kids, your family, and yourself be all you dream you can be.

Careful study and daily practice of CORE Success will provide parents tools to improve their home lives, forge deeper connections, and empower their children. Families that implement CORE Success are thriving rather than faltering, encouraging strong self-esteem for all members, resolving conflict peacefully and respectfully, engaging in dignified and considerate discipline, and abolishing bullying. Parents can enjoy meaningful connection to their kids as they gift them with the power to live peacefully and intentionally.

And in closing, I leave you with this poignant story of old...

A long, long time ago a young Native American boy cowered behind a tree observing a skirmish between his people and the white man. The boy was more than upset; his worldview was tilting. If all he had been taught were true, then how could this type of war happen? He was more than confused, he was scared. In Native cultures the older generation is venerated for its experience and wisdom and, hence, is sought out by the youth for advice and insight. And so this child went in search of his grandfather.

As he approached, he kneeled silently before the man and waited in the stillness until he was acknowledged by the elder. After a period of silence the grandfather spoke. "My son, what is in your heart? What troubles you?" The boy answered, "Grandfather, you have taught me that all people carry goodness inside of them, and that there is no exception to that. I hear and see that there are people who are warring with one another. Our own people are fighting brutally against the white man and against each other. How can that be, Grandfather, when each of us carries goodness within us?"

The grandfather closed his eyes and took his time to respond. Slowly, he opened his eyes and looked down at the earnest face of his grandson. He understood too well the confusion, the hope, and the fear the child felt. Finally, the elder said to him, "In the heart of every human being there live two wolves: the wolf of war which lives in fear, and the wolf of peace which lives in love." The wise man then fell silent.

The youth thought deeply about this answer, yet it led him into even more confusion. He didn't see his question answered. He probed on. "But Grandfather that means endless war, does it not?" he asked.

"It doesn't have to," replied the grandfather.

The boy worked the problem some more. "If there is to be no war, one of the wolves must lead and reign supreme," the young boy replied.

"Indeed," answered the grandfather.

"But how is it decided which of these two wolves will then rule if they both live within our heart?" asked the bewildered child.

The boy's grandfather touched one hand to his heart, and with the other hand open replied, "The wolf that will reign in a person's heart is the one that is nurtured and fed most."

APPENDIX

Bullying is . . .

Bullying can be described as intimidating or threatening behavior toward a weaker person. It can be easily identified as being one-sided, unfair, and often repeated. An uneven distribution of power always exists between the person who bullies and the person who is bullied (this is what clearly distinguishes it from conflict). Bullying behaviors include physically hurting or threatening to hurt someone, repetitive insults and name-calling, derogatory gossip and rumors, social exclusion, and sexual bullying. People who bully thrive on the sense of power and control they get from their bullying behaviors.

Children's Rights and Responsibilities

Right	Responsibility
To have a meal.	To help set the table. Ask if your help is needed with cooking. Help clear your place, the table, the kitchen after a meal.

Right	Responsibility
To live in a peaceful setting.	To live, work, and move respectfully when alone or with others at home.
To have your belongings and property respected.	To care for and return belongings and property of others.
To be safe.	To behave safely—no threatening, pushing, kicking, punching, or fighting.
To be listened to.	To be quiet and listen when others are speaking. To not interrupt others.
To live in a clean environment.	To clean up after yourself.
To feel respected and cared for.	To speak kindly to others—no teasing, bullying, or saying things that are unkind.

Criteria for a Good Rule

- It is clear, specific, and simply stated so that all can understand.
- It states what is permitted as well as what is not permitted
- It is easy to distinguish whether or not the rule has been broken.
- It is respectful and maintains a person's dignity.

Ex-haling Experiences Story

A girl named Martha is still lying in bed 3 minutes after her alarm goes off. All of a sudden her mother calls to her, "Martha, you lazy good for nothing, get your body out of bed now!" (air out). She goes to brush her teeth and her older sister who has already locked herself in the bathroom, says, "Get lost you little creep!" (air out)

When she comes downstairs, her parents are in an ill mood. "You look like a street urchin. There's no way you're going to school dressed so sloppily." She has to go upstairs and change clothes. Now her cereal is totally soggy and she is running late. When she gets to the bus stop, she is called names by a student (air out). Walking into the classroom an older student gives her a shove, her books go flying, and she is made fun of for being clumsy (air out). (Continue with "air out" as you see fit for the story...)

When the teacher calls on her, it becomes apparent that in her morning rush she forgot her homework. Hence, she gets a bad mark for not having done it. When she is then asked to read a text out loud to the class, she makes a mistake in reading and all the kids laugh.

Finally outside for recess, she looks for someone to play with. There seems to be no one around. She asks to join a game and is the last to be picked to play on a kickball team.

On her way home from school the same kids from the bus stop keep teasing her and she runs home in tears.

Luckily today she has ballet practice, which she loves. She arrives in the studio feeling a bit worn. It is dress rehearsal and she has forgotten her costume. She makes a number of mistakes, which, since the recital is tomorrow, brings her teacher and the other dancers down on her pretty hard.

After dinner, when her dad gets home from work, he yells at her for not having done her chore of taking out the trash, saying, "You will never amount to anything. I can never depend on you to do what you're asked to."

At the end of the day, Martha lays in bed staring at the ceiling. She wonders how she could be such a rotten kid, when she tries so hard. Her self-esteem is completely deflated.

Growing in Responsibility

Answer the questions.

1. What do you have responsibility for at home?

_____

_____

2. What do you have responsibility for at school?

_____

_____

3. As you observe yourself, what do you find?

   a. I am most responsible when it comes to:

_____

_____

b. I am not so responsible when it comes to:

_____

_____

4. In general, how responsible do you feel you are (check one).

____ Very responsible
____ Dependable most of the time
____ Only fairly responsible
____ Not too responsible

5. If you feel that you need to improve, tell how you plan to do this.

_____

_____

_____

_____

_____

_____

6. Is being responsible important? Why or why not?

_____

_____

What happened is...

Name: _____Date: _____

Today I (explain what happened)

_____

_____

This was disruptive because / broke the family rule that states

_____

_____

I could have (what could you have done differently for a different outcome?)

_____

_____

What will help me most to change this behavior is

_____

_____

Next time I will

_____

_____

I've learned that

_____

_____

Parent's comments

_____

_____

Child's signature

_____

Is It Safe?

When you are deciding whether it is safe to refuse, ask yourself the following questions:

- Is the person bullying you older or bigger than you are?
- Is more than one person bullying you?
- Do you have any friends nearby who will help you?
- How far away is the nearest adult?
- Do you feel confident enough to stand up to the person(s) who is bullying you?
- Do you think refusing on your own will work?
- Do you feel trapped?
- Is this situation safe or unsafe?

Is This Bullying?

Directions: Place a "B" next to the situations that you think depict bullying behaviors.

1. _____ At recess a big kid keeps pushing down a little kid on purpose.
2. _____ A group of kids always leaves out the new student during soccer games even when she asks to play.
3. _____ Best friends Lisa and Janice argue about whose turn it is during a Monopoly game. Lisa insists she's right.
4. _____ Tim gets angry and calls John a name because he did not come to his birthday party.
5. _____ Some kids take Shane's bat and toss it around on the school bus and won't give it back. Shane tells them to stop, but they don't listen.
6. _____ Laura gets a text from the girl in front of her in math class that says she's dumb.
7. _____ Three kids always make fun of Ben because he wears glasses. This makes him cry.
8. _____ A group of girls chase Justin at recess and try to kiss him even though he has told them he doesn't like it.
9. _____ Joey and Mark arm wrestle a lot. One day Joey's arm gets hurt.
10. _____ Ross snaps Joan's bra at the water fountain every chance he gets.
11. _____ A group of boys on the football team frequently have public Facebook discussions saying a boy on their team is gay and that's the only reason he's on the team.
12. _____ Eighth grade girls and boys call a seventh grade girl sexually graphic names every day at the school bus stop.
13. _____ A sixth grade girl circulates a note saying that Sarah likes a certain boy in the class.
14. _____ Sherri knows Jenny is afraid of spiders. She puts a spider in Jenny's book bag.

Refusing Bullying with Confidence

- Stay cool and calm down.
  - Take deep breaths.
  - Imagine yourself being assertive.
  - Use self-talk.

- Use assertive skills only if you feel the situation is safe and you feel confident.

    - Stand up straight.
    - Have good eye contact.
    - Speak clearly and sound confident and calm.
    - Respect the rights of others.
    - Know your right to be treated fairly.

- Agree with the person who is bullying you (e.g., "Yeah, you're right, I do look like I have four eyes.").

- Use humor (e.g., "Yeah, I got these pants at the second hand store. I picked up a pair for you.").

- Change the subject (e.g., "Hey, are you going to the game tonight?").

- Flatter the person who is bullying you (e.g., "I saw that great shot you made today in basketball." Or "Man, I've wanted to tell you that Mary really likes you. Check her out!").

- Use trickery. Pretend you're sick, pretend to faint, or pretend that your older brother who's a cop/trained in martial arts is picking you up.

- Ask for advice (e.g., "I was wondering if you could tell me where you got those cool sneakers?").

- Make friends. Treat the person who is bullying you as a friend—not as an enemy.

- Try to reason and talk it out with her. Show empathy and try to understand why the person is acting that way.

- Ignore and walk away. The person who is bullying is seeking attention. Say no to being bullied. Make a statement like, "That talk is so uncool. Later!"

- Refuse to fight, no matter what happens. Fighting will just make matters worse.

- Give up your possessions. If the situation is dangerous then it would be smart to give the person who is bullying what they want.

- Scream/yell. If the situation is dangerous, yell out or scream to distract the person who is bullying you. Then you can get away to get help.

- Walk away and get help from a friend or adult—a parent, teacher, police officer, or someone you trust.

Remember that these strategies will not work in every situation. Select the appropriate strategy to use in certain situations. Ask yourself, will this strategy likely work in this situation?

Role-Plays: Dealing with Feelings

Role-Play # 1

You invite a friend to your house for a sleepover. At the last minute your friend calls and says he can't come because his whole family is going out. Later you take a walk and go past your friend's house. The lights are on and the car is in front of the house, so you know they are home. You see the bikes of two of your other friends in front of his house.

Role-Play # 2

Your uncle gave you some money for your birthday. The next day at school you bought ice cream for your friends. The next thing you know, Ryan is telling everyone that you stole the ice cream money out of his desk.

Role-Play # 3

When you get to school, all of your friends are looking at party invitations from one of your classmates. When you look in your desk, there isn't one for you. You always thought you were friends with the person giving the party.

Role-Play # 4

A group of girls all like the same fancy bed pillow in the store window. Stephanie's dad bought her the pillow after she tells him how great it will look in her room. Jill tells all the girls that

Stephanie only bought the pillow to show off and be the first in the group to buy it.

Sense of a Goose

Next fall, when you see geese heading south for the winter, flying along in V formation, you might consider what science has discovered as to why they fly that way. As each bird flaps its wings, it creates an uplift for the bird immediately following. By flying in a V formation, the whole flock adds at least 71 percent greater flying range than if each bird flew on its own.

People who share a common direction and sense of community can get where they are going more quickly and easily because they are traveling on the thrust of one another.

When a goose falls out of the formation, it suddenly feels the drag and resistance of trying to go it alone – and quickly gets back into formation to take advantage of the lifting power of the bird in front.

If we have as much sense as a goose, we will stay in formation with those people who are headed the same way we are.

When the head goose gets tired, it rotates back in the wing and another goose flies point.

It is sensible to take turns doing demanding jobs, whether with people or with geese flying south.

Geese honk from behind to encourage those up front to keep up their speed.

What message do we give when we honk from behind?

Finally—and this is important—when a goose gets sick or is wounded by a gunshot, and falls out of formation, two other geese fall out with that goose and follow it down to lend help and protection. They stay with the fallen goose until it is able to fly, or until it dies; and only then do they launch out on their own, or with another formation to catch up with their group.

If we have the sense of a goose, we will stand by each other like that.

Author unknown

Should I Refuse or Report?

Read each of the following situations. Decide whether you would refuse the bullying on your own or report the incident to an adult. Be prepared to explain your reasoning.

Situation	Refuse	Report	Not sure	Both
The biggest student in your class stops you at the bus stop. She demands your homework. If you don't give up your homework she threatens to pound you.				
You used to be good friends with three classmates, but you had a disagreement. Now they leave you out of activities and ignore you. They have been spreading rumors about you on Facebook.				
A bigger kid from another class has been following you around during recess for a couple of days. He has been laughing at you and making fun of you. He already knocked you down and kicked you.				
You are a new student at school. Several kids in your class make fun of you. When you walk by some of your classmates, they snicker, giggle, point at you, and whisper to each other.				
You are alone in the washroom at lunch-time. Three kids who are known to bully students came in and started making fun of you and pushing you around.				

Situation	Refuse	Report	Not sure	Both
You're new to the volleyball team. During the third week of practice, you find out other teammates have been writing insulting posts about you on Facebook for the last 3 weeks.				
You are wearing shorts to school. You are playing basketball during recess with some other kids. Just as you jump to make a shot, someone pulls down your shorts and exposes your underwear. The other kids laugh and point at you.				

Tattling vs. Reporting

Tattling

When someone tattles or tells on someone who has done something, the purpose is to get attention and/or to get that person into trouble. The primary focus is not to help someone. This is informing unnecessarily.

Reporting

When someone reports an incident, the purpose is to keep themselves and others safe. The intention is to help someone.

Reporting may be difficult but it may be the only way to help stop bullying. Adults must know about bullying before they can do anything to help.

How to Report Bullying

Think about these points:

- Who are you going to report bullying to? Parents, teacher, relative, police, etc.
- Decide how you're going to report the bullying—verbally or in writing.
- Decide on an appropriate time and place to report bullying.

- When reporting tell:
- Who was involved.
- When it happened.
- Where it happened.
- What happened.

Remember, if the bullying doesn't stop, <u>report it again</u>.

The Weight of a Snowflake

"Tell me the weight of a snowflake," a coal-mouse asked a wild dove.

"Nothing more than nothing," was the answer.

"In that case, I must tell you a marvelous story," the coal-mouse said. "I sat on the branch of a fir, close to its trunk, when it began to snow ... not heavily, not in a raging blizzard ... no, just like in a dream, without a wound, and without any violence. Since I did not have anything better to do, I counted the snowflakes settling on the twigs and needles of my branch. Their number was exactly 3,741,952. When the 3,741,953rd dropped onto the branch, nothing more than nothing, as you say ... the branch broke off."

Having said that the coal-mouse flew away.

The dove, since Noah's time an authority on the matter, thought about the story for a while and finally said to herself, "Perhaps there is only one person's voice lacking for peace to come to the world."

By Kurt Kauter from *New Fables; Thus spoke the Marabou*

What Can I Do?

Recognize the Bullying.

- Ask yourself...
- Is it harmful and/or threatening behavior?
- Is it one-sided?
- Is it unfair?
- Do you feel unsafe?

Refuse the Bullying.

- Decide whether it is safe to refuse on your own.
- Stay calm.

- Decide what strategies to use.
- If it is unsafe to refuse on your own, or it doesn't work, report the bullying and get help from an adult.

Prevent Bullying from happening to you.

- Stay close to friends.
- Make smart decisions.
- Stay in sight of peers and adults when possible.
- Don't be alone in places where you may be bullied.
- Don't set yourself up to be bullied.
- Don't provoke others or make situations worse.
- Don't brag about having money or expensive or special items.

Develop your own self-confidence.

- Get involved in something that makes you feel good about yourself.
- Build solid friendships and/or join a team (see Chapter 3, *Living to Thrive*).
- Advocate for others when you see bullying happening, or get help and report it.

When I'm angry ...

I will take the time to accept how I am feeling right now.

I will listen to my body, to how I'm feeling, and where I feel it in my body.

I will calm down because that feels better than staying upset. I can calm myself down by taking deep breaths, counting slowly, thinking positive, thinking calming thoughts, listening to music, going for a walk, using self-talk (e.g., As long as I keep my cool, I'm in control; Let's work this out, maybe she has a point).

I will try to understand how the other person is feeling, what they may be thinking, and why. I can try and figure out how this could have happened.

I will think of a plan of how to solve this problem. (Use self-talk or write it down.) What can I do? What would I like the other person to do? What kind of help, or whose help, can I get in order to solve this?

References

Chapter 1: Home Is a Haven

Oxford University Press. (1997). *The New Oxford Dictionary of English.* Oxford University Press.

Dooley, M. (2015). *Thoughts become things. @TUT.com.* Retrieved from: http://www.tut.com/Inspiration/nftu

Chapter 2: The CORE Success of Parenting

Winkel, S., Petermann, F., Petermann, U. (2006). *Lernpsychologie.* Stuttgart: UTB Basics.

Chapter 3: Living to Thrive

Berk, L. S., Felten, D. L., Tan, S. A., Bittman, B. B., and Westengard, J. (2001). *Modulation of neuroimmune parameters during laughter.* Alternative Therapies 7(2):62–76. Retrieved from: http://web.missouri.edu/~segerti/3830/Humorhealth.pdf

Birch, S. H., and Ladd, G. W. (1997). The teacher–child relationship and children's early school adjustment. *Journal of School Psychology* 35(1):61–79.

Christakis, D. A. (2009). *The effects of infant media usage: what do we know and what should we learn?* Acta Paediatrica 98:8–16. Retrieved from: http://echd430-f13-love. wikispaces.umb.edu/file/view/Pediatrics+article.pdf

Council on Communications and Media. (2009). *Media violence.* Pediatrics 124(5):1495–1503. Retrieved from: http:// pediatrics.aappublications.org/content/124/5/1495.full

Kozeis, N. (2009). *Impact of computer use on children's vision.* Hippokratia 13(4):230–231. Retrieved from: http://www. ncbi.nlm.nih.gov/pmc/articles/PMC2776336/

Kubey, R., and Csikszentmihalyi, M. (2003). *Television addiction is no mere metaphor.* Scientific American Mind 202:48–55.

Retrieved from: http://www.simpletoremember.com/ vitals/TVaddictionIsNoMereMetaphor.pdf

Liedloff, J. (1986). *The Continuum Concept: In Search of Happiness Lost*. Boston: DeCapo Press.

Waldman, M., Nicholson, S., and Adilov, N. (2006). *Does television cause autism?* NBER Working Paper No. 12632. Retrieved from: http://www.nber.org/papers/w12632

Chapter 4: Raising Self-Esteem

Rogers, C. (1977). *Carl Rogers on Personal Power*. New York: Delacorte Press.

Chapter 5: Discipline with Dignity

Covey, S. (1989). *Seven Habits of Highly Effective People*. New York: Free Press.

Oxford University Press. (1998). *The New Oxford Dictionary of English*. New York: Oxford University Press.

Chapter 6: Resolving Conflict

Cierpke, M. (2005). *FAUSTLOS–Ein Curriculum zur Foerderung sozialer Kompetenzen und zur Praevention von aggressivem und gewaltbereitem Verhalten bei Kindern*. Praxis der Kinderpsychologie und Kinderpsychiatrie 46(3):236–247. Retrieved from: http://psydok.sulb.uni-saarland.de/volltexte/2012/3974/pdf/46.19973_10_39749.pdf_new.pdf

Nolting, H. P. (1993). *Aggression und Gewalt*. Munich: Verlag W. Kohlhammer.

Chapter 7: Abolishing Bullying

Belson, K. (2014). *New Giant John Jerry unlikely to be barred for bullying, Coughlin says*. The New York Times, March 26, 2014. Retrieved from: http://www.nytimes.com/2014/03/27/sports/football/coughlin-doubts-john-jerry-will-be-suspended-for-bullying-role.html?ref=topics&_r=1

Bureau of Justice Statistics. (2006). *Indicators of School Crime and Safety*. Westlake Village, CA: National School Safety

Center. Retrieved from: https://docs.google.com/view
er?a=v&pid=sites&srcid=c2Nob29sc2FmZXR5XR5Ln
VzfG5zc2N8Z3g6MTI5ZDNmOGRlMmI0MzRhZA
Kaplan, K. (2014). *Victims of bullying live with the consequences for decades, study says*. Los Angeles Times. Retrieved from http://articles.latimes.com/2014/apr/22/sports/la-sp-ducks-stars-20140423
Lush, T. (2013). *Rebecca Ann Sedwick bullied for months before suicide, sheriff says*. Huffington Post Retrieved from http://www.huffingtonpost.com/2013/09/13/rebecca-ann-sedwick_n_3922738.html?utm_hp_ref=school-bullying
UCLA Department of Psychology. (n.d.). *Common Psychosocial Problems of School Aged Youth: Developmental Variations, Problems, Disorders and Perspectives for Prevention and Treatment*. Los Angeles: Center of Mental Health in Schools. Retrieved from: http://smhp.psych.ucla.edu/pdfdocs/psysocial/entirepacket.pdf

Organizations
Worth Contacting

The following is only a small handful of the many groups that are actively and positively supporting youth, family and human values:

Global Peace Foundation

https://www.globalpeace.org
+1 – 202 – 643–4733

Mercy Corp–Conflict Management Group

http://www.mercycorps.org
+1 – 888 – 747- 7440

Option Institute International Learning and Training Center

http://www.option.org
1- 800 – 714–2779

Peace in Schools Project

http://www.peaceinschools.org
+1 – 971 – 800–0471

Positive Coaching Alliance

https://www.positivecoach.org
+ 1 – 866 – 725 – 0024

The Virtues Project

http://www.virtuesproject.org
+1 – 888 – 261–5611

World Vision–Youth Empowerment Program

http://www.worldvision.org/get-involved/
youth-empowerment-program
+ 1 – 888 – 511–6548

Notes of Gratitude

Any valuable work is built on the shoulders of many who have gone before us and from whom we have learned. My thanks here cannot express my gratitude to those who have helped me give birth to this work, and to myself:

Shirley Everett, master educator, role model, creator of *Learning Peace – On the Road to a Peaceful School*, my collaborator and dear friend without whom this work would never have come to be.

Detlef Steindorf for joining with me in learning to parent with intention, connection, and unconditional love.

Natalie Rogers, humanistic psychologist, pioneer in person-centered art therapy and mentor, for showing me the transformational power of understanding another human being.

Landmark Education and all of its amazing teaching.

Barry and Samahria Kaufman, Beverly and Clyde Haberman, and Raun Kaufman of The Option Institute for providing me the tools and teaching that helped me transform myself out of limiting beliefs into a life of sovereignty, love and full of happiness.

Steve Harrison, Martha Bullen, Geoffery Berwind and the entire Bradley Communications team for helping me make my Quantum Leap.

Magdalena Gerlach, Claudia Stein-Carr, Allyson Bishop, and Liz Zawada who always believe in me, who held me up and who cheer me on.

Rita Reinhardt and Melanie Carlone for loving me unconditionally.

Robert Angelo Carlone, my way-shower, for living an exemplary life of integrity, boldness, dauntlessness and service.

Above all, Dominik Tyler and Leah Lorén, who thankfully chose me as their mother, who have always called me to be the highest version of myself, and whose purity of heart taught me to believe, without a doubt, in the goodness in each and every one of us, including myself.

About the Author

Leeza Carlone Steindorf

Empowering people to see and express the excellence and success they already possess at their core excites me. Since 2002, I have been facilitating organizational, educational, personal, and professional development internationally. I am an expert in parenting methodologies, conflict management systems, and communication strategies, hold numerous professional certifications and accreditations, and a degree in business management.

My life and work have been profoundly influenced by the humanistic Rogerian model of psychology. I had the honor of interpreting for and assisting for years Dr. Natalie Rogers, Carl Rogers' colleague and daughter, in person-centered therapy trainings in Europe. My professional certifications include: Mediator, Trainer and Group Facilitator, Business and Life Coach and as a somatic education specialist of the Feldenkrais Method.

I enjoy exploring cutting-edge new thought and quantum physics, practicing mindfulness, and am a passionate runner and dancer. Born and raised in glorious Colorado, I've spent all of my adult life living and working in Europe and have spent time in over 37 countries on this amazing planet. My international mindset infuses my life and work in a powerful way. I am truly a global citizen and pledge my allegiance to this sacred planet we call home.

My books and trainings as well as my consulting and keynote speeches draw from my broad and intercultural experience working for corporations and entrepreneurs, educational institutions, school systems, families and young people.

In all I do, I am called to help people connect with themselves and others. I love to use my skills to empower individuals and businesses aspiring to **Clarity. Ownership. Resolution. Excellence.**

These are not just words; they are the heartbeat of my work in transforming human behavior into functional excellence.

Although I love what I do, it is always my family that remains at my center and who inspire the joy that I carry into my day. With them I dance, laugh, travel, explore and celebrate life on this planet. My children have taught me to believe in goodness and have helped me see that true success resides solidly within one's self.

Learn More with Leeza

This work is my joy. I invite you to contact me and take advantage of what I offer. I coach and consult, speak to groups and offer trainings to parents, educators, youth, social organizations and businesses to find their clarity of direction, their passion, and their well-being.

Won't you join me?

- Visit my website for free materials, to hire me as a keynote speaker for your next event, to buy a book, register for an online or live training, or to schedule a live or online session with me at https://coresuccess.com
- Sign up for my blog at https://www.LeezaSteindorf.com
- Follow me on Twitter @LeezaSteindorf
- Visit my Facebook page, ask questions, post comments, and stay in touch. https://www.facebook.com/LeezaCarloneSteindorf and https://www.facebook.com/CoreSuccess/
- Please contact me at Leeza@CoreSuccess.com with comments and experiences you've had with this work. I would love to hear from you. If you have questions, please post them to my Facebook page so I can be sure to answer them for you.
- Post a review on Amazon if this book has been useful to you and your family.

Please know that I honor your path as a parent, wherever you may find yourself on it. It is a glorious and challenging role and the most important one in the life of your children.

Be well, stay happy and thrive!

Made in the USA
San Bernardino, CA
09 January 2017